The Second Cycle

THE SECOND CYCLE
Winning the War Against Bureaucracy

Lars Kolind

Ideas. Action. Impact.
**Wharton School
Publishing**

Vice President, Editor-in-Chief: Tim Moore
Wharton Editor: Yoram (Jerry) Wind
Acquisitions Editor: Paula Sinnott
Editorial Assistant: Susie Abraham
Development Editor: Russ Hall
Associate Editor-in-Chief and Director of Marketing: Amy Neidlinger
Cover Designer: Alan Clements
Managing Editor: Gina Kanouse
Project Editor: Michael Thurston
Copy Editor: Kelli Brooks
Senior Indexer: Cheryl Lenser
Senior Compositor: Gloria Schurick
Manufacturing Buyer: Dan Uhrig

Ideas. Action. Impact.
Wharton School
Publishing

© 2006 by Pearson Education, Inc.
Publishing as Wharton School Publishing
Upper Saddle River, New Jersey 07458

Wharton School Publishing offers excellent discounts on this book when ordered in quantity for bulk purchases or special sales. For more information, please contact U.S. Corporate and Government Sales, 1-800-382-3419, corpsales@pearsontechgroup.com. For sales outside the U.S., please contact International Sales at international@pearsoned.com.

Printed in the United States of America

First Printing: April 2006

ISBN 0-13-173629-9

Pearson Education LTD.
Pearson Education Australia PTY, Limited.
Pearson Education Singapore, Pte. Ltd.
Pearson Education North Asia, Ltd.
Pearson Education Canada, Ltd.
Pearson Educatión de Mexico, S.A. de C.V.
Pearson Education—Japan
Pearson Education Malaysia, Pte. Ltd.

Library of Congress Cataloging-in-Publication Data
Kolind, Lars.
 The second cycle : winning the war against bureaucracy / Lars Kolind.
    p. cm.
 ISBN 0-13-173629-9 (hardback : alk. paper) 1. Industrial management. 2. Success in business. 3. Creative ability in business. I. Title.
 HD31.K5987 2006
 658.4'063—dc22
                          2005034012

To everyone who struggles for their organization to become more relevant and innovative.

CONTENTS

ABOUT THE AUTHOR

Lars Kolind, born in Denmark in 1947, is a mathematician and a leader. He served as director at Denmark's National Research Laboratory from 1981 to 1984, became COO of Radiometer A/S—a world leader in scientific instrumentation—from 1984 to 1988, and was responsible for the dramatic turnaround of troubled hearing aid manufacturer Oticon, which he led to world leadership during his 10 years as CEO from 1988 to 1998.

Kolind is involved in public work within the fields of education and social welfare. He was a founder of The Danish Competency Council, which published the world's first national accounts on human capital in 1999. He also founded The Danish Business Network for Social Cohesion and The Copenhagen Center, a government agency that fosters partnerships between the public and private sectors in Europe to fight social exclusion.

Kolind serves as non-executive board member or chairman of a number of corporations, including world-leading pump manufacturer Grundfos,

Unimerco Group, Scancom International, Zealand Pharma, Kristeligt Dagblad, and BankInvest Ventures. He is a principal of the Q Thought Leader Network and he serves international Scouting as deputy chairman of the board of The World Scout Foundation. Kolind is an adjunct professor of leadership at the Aarhus School of Business. He has received several awards, including Denmark's Man of the Year in 1996, and his work is used as classic management cases at many leading business schools around the world.

PREFACE

During the time I worked on this book in 2005, the news was full of stories about Ford and General Motors selling off assets, labor unions losing members, ever new problems hitting the Catholic Church, public schools being criticized for lack of relevance, German industry unable to meet competition from low-wage countries, the Bush administration stuck in scandals, and numerous other well-established institutions in deep trouble. It seems that everybody accepts that the upward part of the corporate lifecycle must be followed by a downward part that ends with extinction. The Roman Empire, The Soviet Union, The British car industry, Digital Equipment Corporation, Enron, and Arthur Andersen are but a few examples of the corporate lifecycle curve that most people believe is as fundamental to business as Newton's Law of Gravity is to classical physics.

There is little doubt that there are mechanisms associated with success that tend to transform once agile and creative organizations into complacent bureaucracies. However, the big question is why top managers overlook these mechanisms in their own organizations, even at times when their organizations' lack of performance is obvious to outsiders. What is it that blinds management and prevents it from taking appropriate action? Why is this disease allowed to develop for so long that it is often impossible to cure when it has finally been discovered? And what can be done to revert or avoid decline and perhaps even establish a platform for renewed growth, a second cycle?

To find an answer to these questions, I used my personal experience as a starting point. I reflected upon the organizations I had worked for, either as an employee, a manager, a board member, or a volunteer. I searched for small things under the surface that indicated or influenced the mechanisms behind the corporate lifecycles. I was particularly struck by several examples where organizations possessed knowledge, ideas, technologies, or people that could have brought them into the world league of their industry if opportunities had been managed properly; but they never followed those opportunities. I realized that opportunities were most often lost when the organization appeared to be most successful—not when it was in trouble.

This book neither fits into the mold of a conventional management textbook nor is it an autobiography. My experience with conventional management textbooks is that authors often attempt to make something look like a theory that has very little theoretical substance. Simple points that could be conveyed in a minimal amount of text are often explained and illustrated with so much excess text that the message gets lost. On the other hand, autobiographies often seem to serve only one purpose: to celebrate the merits of the author.

I call this an experience-based hands-on management book. It is written for easy reading—not loaded with unnecessary theory and references. It is designed to be useful for managers, politicians, volunteers, students, and others who are involved in or concerned about the future of their organizations. It recognizes current theories of management, but builds primarily on practical experience—that is, what has worked for me. I have not studied the behavior of hundreds of organizations in order to back up my recommendations with solid statistical evidence. However, this has given me more freedom to express my points bluntly and clearly. You will have to determine whether these recommendations apply to your organization.

The book has four parts.

First is an analysis of the mechanism of the conventional corporate lifecycle, in particular, why organizations become stagnate and decline at times when they think they are highly successful.

Second, you will find a proposed design for a new platform for innovation and growth—the second cycle. This platform stands on four pillars and each pillar has its own chapter: meaning, partnership, collaboration, and leadership.

Third, I invite you to look into my toolbox. It contains seven tools that I have used to diagnose an organization, establish a new foundation for it, and move it into a second cycle of sustained innovation and growth.

Fourth, I illustrate the main points of this book with three living examples of organizations that in my view are experiencing severe decline because they have not realized the need to move into a second cycle. I finish by putting the examples into greater perspective: how we could enjoy much more growth and prosperity if mature organizations were able and willing to jump out of their conventional lifecycles and start a new second cycle.

For inspiration, I have enclosed as an appendix the most significant case study I know about organizational transformation: the rebirth of troubled hearing aid manufacturer Oticon into the industry leader in the 1990s. That story taught me about both organizational decline and what it can take to jump into a second cycle. May it inspire you as well.

Throughout this book, I invite you to take a moment and reflect on your own situation or other organizations you know, in light of what you read. Watch for the 🔍 symbol!

—Lars Kolind

ACKNOWLEDGMENTS

The main inspiration for this book came from my work at Oticon from 1988 to 1998. I was part of an inspiring management team that worked its way through a tough turnaround and the subsequent process of building a truly knowledge-based organization. Many employees and managers from Oticon inspired, supported, and encouraged me in this process. It is difficult to acknowledge some over others, but I want to mention especially six people without whom the Oticon transformation could never have succeeded: Steen Davidsen, Torben Petersen, Helle Thorup-Witt, Lars Kirk, Søren Holst, and Niels Jacobsen.

Later, I continued working with design of innovative organizations. I am indebted particularly to Niels Due Jensen, CEO of Grundfos; Kenneth Iversen, CEO of Unimerco; and Eva Steiness, CEO of Zealand Pharma. Klaus J. Jacobs, founder and chairman of K. J. Jacobs Holding and chairman of Adecco, gave me a global perspective on business that went beyond what I had experienced as a CEO.

Many executives and associates have taken part in discussions on the issues in this book. I thank you all for your time and passion. Academically, I have been particularly inspired by Professor Yoram (Jerry) Wind, who gave me his book, *The Power of Impossible Thinking* (Wharton, 2005), exactly at the time I needed a language to express mental models of organizations. Niels Christian Nielsen, founder of Q Network Inc., opened my eyes to the theory of knowledge management, and Mette Laursen, founder of LinKS, inspired me to work on learning and coaching. Klaus Fog, founder and chairman of Sigma Partners, helped me understand the greater perspective of the work, and Alan Webber, founder of Fast Company, helped me see the big picture in what I was doing. I am indebted to the late Bent Rieneck, from the Danish Defense Management Institute, who 20 years ago taught me how to establish consensus in an organization using his so-called "dialogue shop" concept. I have developed his method further into the CCCP tool, which can be found in Chapter 7, "The Toolbox."

My family has been a source of great inspiration and support. My wife, Vibeke Riemer, and our four children, Kristian, Torsten, Jens, and Astrid, never turned down an opportunity to discuss findings and concepts. It is never easy to be married to a person that is struggling with a manuscript for almost a year. I am thankful to Vibeke for continuously supporting this project. My brother, Peder, challenged my thinking and provided valuable comments and constant encouragement in the writing process.

CHAPTER 1

The First Cycle: Why Success Breeds Failure

LIFECYCLES FOLLOW THE WAY PEOPLE THINK

The history of business is paved with companies where roaring success was followed by steep decline: Digital Equipment Corporation, MG-Rover, and Upjohn, just to mention a few. Steep decline followed decades of prosperous growth and industry leadership. It seems as though a virus was allowed to enter into the once-healthy businesses. The virus gradually spread without management or staff really bothering or even knowing what happened. Alarm signals were overheard or neglected for years. Management continued to act as if the company was successful, even at a point where the emerging disaster was obvious to outsiders.

That's how a company's lifecycle usually goes: It begins with a period of struggle before the business takes off. Then, there is a period of rapid and prosperous growth with frequent new product introductions, growing market shares, and high customer satisfaction. After this growth period, a period of stagnation often follows, in which management is under increasing pressure. Consultants are brought in and management is changed, followed by painful downsizings that temporarily restore profitability. Mergers and acquisitions are used to create new growth and profits through cost savings from elimination of double functions.

But the capability of the business to continue the former organic growth seems to have disappeared. Despite apparent financial success, the lifecycle is about to turn into a death cycle. Additional management changes, additional downsizings, and additional mergers fail to address the key issue: The company has lost the innovative capability, the focus, and the energy that originally made it successful. Subsequent downsizings lead to corporate anorexia: The organization becomes leaner and weaker.

Companies die from this process, either from being taken over by others or simply by going out of business. The first lifecycle becomes the last. The lifecycle becomes a death cycle.

This book is about breaking the stagnation or downturn of the first cycle and turning it into a second cycle. It helps you understand if you are actually in danger of being caught in the downward cycle. It suggests how you can create a new platform for a second cycle and how you can move the existing organization from the first into the second cycle.

Cycles are determined by the way people in general, and managers in particular, think. To understand why, you need to look upon the way people think.

Imagine you are driving your car on the way to an important meeting. You take an alternative route with very little traffic to play it safe. You have enough time, but not too much. Suddenly, there is a smell from something obviously burned or at least very hot. Within a split second, your brain builds what is called a mental model of the situation, building upon your experience from previous situations and your current situation. How far do you still have to go? How much time do you have? What happened last time you had a burned smell from your car? Where can you get a taxi?

Your mental model of the situation is built on very limited actual information: the smell of something burned. But you add all sorts of other information from past experience to provide you with the relevant framework to analyze the situation and to act. You have stopped thinking about what you will say at the upcoming meeting. Not even 10 percent of your mental energy is devoted to that any more. You have changed your mental model 100 percent, from thinking about today's meeting to dealing with the smell issue. After a few minutes of driving, you stop the car. Very cautiously, you open the hood to find out how serious the trouble is. Will the motor catch fire?

After a little search, you realize that the smell comes from a few leaves that somehow have entered the motor at a hot spot. The leaves are almost burned and there seems nothing left to be concerned about.

Now your *mental model* immediately switches back to the situation before you discovered the smell: You now think of the meeting, the people you will talk to, and the contract you hope to land. A new mental model has entered once again based on very limited information, but drawing on vast reservoirs of knowledge from your brain. Again, this new mental model doesn't share the attention of your mind 80 percent or so. One mental model at a time dominates your thinking 100 percent.

Mental models determine the way people think and act. They enable us to switch very quickly from one situation to the other. We don't need to gather detailed information about the actual situation because the brain simply chooses a mental model, downloads it, and starts to use it.

Despite quick access, mental models have been built over long periods of time. The more times you have faced a specific type of situation, the more you have developed your relevant mental model.

Organizations have mental models, too, especially successful organizations. Organizations tend to remember their successes and failures. The more successes they experience, the more aspects and nuances they add to their mental model. They remember the development of a very successful product and how they surprised competition with a unique marketing concept. They remember how a group of engineers came up with a new technology that boosted performance of the company's product, and they don't forget the managers that came from another industry thinking they could change this industry without fully understanding it.

Organizational memory is the foundation for their mental model. It defines their success formula, such as "The H-P Way," and it determines their reactions to problems and opportunities. It guides their thinking and defines their horizon. The more successful the organization is, the stronger its mental model becomes.

As an illustration, let us go back and take a look at how the mental model of my former company, Oticon, emerged in the 1970s and 1980s.[1]

HOW OTICON BECAME DEAF

In the 1960s, Oticon was a small local hearing aid manufacturer serving primarily local and regional markets with Denmark as its home base. Denmark, however, had a unique combination of three factors that were found nowhere else in the world:

- Research within the field of sound had reached a world-leading level at the Technical University of Denmark.
- Ear, nose, and throat (ENT) doctors at Danish hospitals were highly focused on better hearing care to their patients in addition to cost-effective care. This was unlike doctors in other countries, such as the United Kingdom, that focused almost entirely on cost reduction within hearing care. In other words, Denmark's doctors went for greater value, whereas most others went for cost reduction.
- The Danish government was willing to publicly subsidize treatment for hearing loss at Danish hospitals—unlike any other country in the world at that time.

The three small Danish hearing aid manufacturers were quick to take advantage of this situation and competed fiercely to develop higher performing and more reliable products to serve the needs of

---

[1] You can find the full Oticon case study in the appendix at the end of this book. It includes both the growth and decline parts of the first cycle and the subsequent turn-around that led to Oticon's second cycle.

the Danish hearing care service, whereas hundreds of manufacturers in the rest of the world were mainly focused on cost reduction.

Within two decades, the three Danish manufacturers—and Oticon in particular—had won positions on the list of the 10 largest manufacturers in the world, enjoying a combined market share of more than 30 percent of the world market.

Oticon was the most successful of the three, and company sales and profits skyrocketed. The company grew to more than 1,000 employees in about 10 countries. The four directors were seen as gurus, and salaries, pension schemes, offices, and company cars reached a level that was perceived as suitable for a world-leading business. The first cycle was at its steep growing stage.

It was in this period that Oticon's mental model emerged. Oticon's mental model perceived hearing aids as standard hardware products to be manufactured in large series in their highly automated plants. It looked upon users as patients with little choice, which was the reality those days. The choice of hearing aid was a professional one, made by audiologists and hearing aid dispensers, not by consumers. Oticon's mental model rightly perceived acoustical performance as the key criterion for choosing one hearing aid over the other.

Oticon was the master that took the lead in moving hearing aids from the pocket to behind the ear—a great achievement, marketing-wise and technologically. The behind-the-ear mental model of the 1970s was indeed a winning formula for Oticon.

But customers wanted to move to the next stage: They wanted hearing aids to move into the ear and the ear canal, a distance of less than an inch. However, this move was difficult from two points of view: Space in the ear was much smaller than behind the ear and worse, the shape of ear canals differed tremendously from person to person. That required the behind-the-ear mass-produced product to become a customized one. The market moved from mass production to mass customization.

Oticon stuck to its mental model despite the apparent change in the marketplace. Oticon honestly thought that consumers were wrong. Consumers didn't understand what was good for them. And professionals seemed to be so hungry for business that they accepted the demand for inferior in-the-ear products.

Oticon started to lose business. In Oticon's mental model, there was only one logical response: to develop even more superior behind-the-ear products so that the acoustical quality difference would be so obvious that nobody would choose an in-the-ear hearing aid any more. Oticon started to refine and improve its outdated mental and business model. It defended its current mental model by prescribing more of the same. More of what it was good at: high performance, behind-the-ear hearing aids.

More and more salespeople were unhappy. They reported back reactions from dissatisfied audiologists that threatened to stop doing business with Oticon if Oticon did not enter the in-the-ear segment. They perceived Oticon to be arrogant. Oticon management fought back by ordering the salespeople not to waste their time talking like competitors. They should instead go out and sell the Oticon advantage to audiologists.

Oticon continued to defend and improve its irrelevant mental model for almost 10 years. And when the headwind became too strong, Oticon's entrance into in-the-ear hearing aids was only half-hearted.

Even at the time when custom-built in-the-ear products had captured half of the world market, Oticon maintained that the market was wrong and the whole thing would blow over.

It didn't.

Finally, Oticon's response was to develop a mass-produced, standard, in-the-ear product that needed no customization—that is, a behind-the-ear product to be clicked directly on to the ear mold. Sound was fine, but it looked nothing but terrible and the market completely rejected it and bought the customized products instead.

Oticon lost market share, but continued to blame the competition and the customers. It was only when the company lost about half of its equity in one year (1987) that the board finally realized that something radical had to be done. The upward part of Oticon's first lifecycle had lasted about 75 years. The downward part, or death cycle, had lasted almost 10 years. During the first eight or nine years of the death cycle, management still had the illusion that the company was on the upward trend. It had no idea that below the surface of success, Oticon was heading directly into bankruptcy and extinction.

The board of directors' diagnosis was that the company needed a strong leader that could reduce costs and restore profitability. It prescribed more power and authority.

There is no question that Oticon needed power and authority, but the real issue was different: how to reinstall hearing into a deaf company. In other words, how to make a conservative company innovative and flexible, how to carry through a paradigm shift, and how to break the first cycle and build a platform for a possible second cycle.

Oticon was an extreme example. It should have been obvious to management that something was fundamentally wrong. But even in such an extreme case, Oticon management—then the dream team of the industry—did not realize that its mental model was becoming irrelevant.

 Reflect for a moment. Could your organization be in the middle of exactly the same development without management having a clue? Hopefully, your organization has not progressed too far into the phases of decay so that you have time to take the necessary steps; and hopefully, this book can inspire you to find out where you are. Remember that it is not only managers of the hearing-aid businesses who lose their hearing; the mechanism is the same and the need to challenge your mental model is no less important for any industry.

THREE FACTORS THAT TURN THE LIFECYCLE CURVE

Companies are caught by the cycle on their way up, not on the way down. It is when success is celebrated that the virus of arrogance enters the body. When a CEO speaks enthusiastically about "The Company Way" or "Our Recipe for Success," he or she opens the company up for a virus that may be fatal five or 10 years later.

That is the virus that turns the direction of the organizational lifecycle.

Three basic factors eventually turn the lifecycle curve for organizations into a death cycle: size, age, and success. Table 1-1 shows how the mechanism functions.

Table 1-1 How Organizations Get on the Downward Track

Success:	Leads to more:	With the consequence that:	But the organization continues to blame others:	...Which in the end leads to decline and:
Successful growth over time involves three basic factors:	Management layers.	Management loses touch with customers and grassroots.	Competition that has become much more intense this year.	Less action. Slower action.
	Departments.			
■ Size. ■ Age. ■ Success.	Formalized procedures.	Information gets delayed and filtered.	Customers that have changed preferences to much cheaper products.	More of the same action—that is, less innovation.
	Long-range planning.			
	Budgeting.	Arrogance prevents management from taking challenges seriously.	The rise or fall of the U.S. dollar. The emergence of low-cost suppliers from Asia. Unions that demand higher wages and expensive health schemes.	
	Reports.			
	Meetings.			
	Coordination.			
	Suboptimization.			
	Traditions.			
	"Our way" mentality.			
	Internal friction.			
	Intrigue.			

Before we go into each of the driving forces, think for a moment about your own organization:

- Where do you think your organization is on its lifecycle curve?
- Have you ever heard management discuss this question?
- Are the employees as satisfied as management with the current state of affairs?
- Do customers feel that your organization is as service minded and flexible as management thinks it is?

If your answers to these questions indicate that your organization might need a wake-up call, you are not alone. My experience is that most organizations need it, in particular, those that have grown beyond 100 employees, those that are more than 10 years of age, and those that have been reasonably successful with what they do.

SIZE

As organizations grow, they tend to become more fragmented. They need more management levels, more specialized departments, more middle managers, more executives, more staff functions, more assistants and support functions, and larger corporate headquarters.

This fragmentation introduces filters between decision makers and where the action is. In small businesses, the owners and leaders know every single customer, small and large. They hear about every single complaint and they also meet satisfied customers that tell them what the customers like about the company. They know every single employee and probably their families. They are close to where the rubber meets the road.

In a larger business, there are departments that take care of every aspect of customer relations: marketing and sales, delivery, customer service, finance, and communication. And most top managers consider their primary role to be managing the whole company rather than interfering with any specific department. Customers become statistics or numbers. Satisfied customers show up as percentages in surveys. Dissatisfied customers are counted as quality costs. Customers' ideas for product modifications or innovations may be picked up by salespeople, but rarely make their way out of the sales department.

All of this leads to a longer distance between the places of the "real business," where the company meets the customer, and management. Information from the market does not reach management at all, or may only reach management in a refined form—for example, in statistics. In the filtering and refinement process, the essence of information is often lost. In particular, this is because those that do the filtering and processing tend to convey that part of the original information that they believe management wants to hear or see.

AGE

As organizations grow older, they develop traditions. It is not only that they conduct the New Year's reception exactly like last year, which is highly visible. But organizations also develop their specific ways of communicating internally, a culture of conflict handling or avoiding, and a tradition for dealing with new ideas that may be much less visible. Many such traditions are not even recognized as specific to the company—they are just the natural ways we do things around here.

Traditions may be very important, despite the fact that they are invisible. If there is a tradition for lack of communication between the sales department and research and development, one day products will tend to meet the engineers' needs rather than the customers' needs. Age gives tradition preference over innovation. And the older the company gets, the stronger the preference for tradition gets.

SUCCESS

Success is the most dangerous factor, however, because success inevitably leads to self-satisfaction. The more successful organizations become, the happier they are with the way they currently do things. "The H-P Way" or the "Siemens Spirit" reflects pride and happiness with the way things are. They are mental models that once were successful, but are not necessarily successful any more.

Only rarely do organizations know concretely the true source of their current success. Customer surveys may indicate that superb product design is a strong factor, but in reality, formulas of success are more often a combination of multiple factors that don't show up in surveys. In particular, soft factors very rarely come up—for example, management style, fundamental company values and their interpretation, or a unique interplay within a group of key people. And long after that unique point has gone away, the organization continues to believe that it possesses the secret key to success. The organization continues to perceive that it is still on the upward part of the lifecycle curve, and it often takes a dramatic crisis to uncover the reality.

Such companies may well show growing sales and profits, but rarely through the dramatic organic growth that once created their success. Mature businesses often enjoy massive positive cash flow from their original (cash cow) core business. These cash flows tend to be spent outside of the core business with the result that the core business is milked to a degree that leaves too little for the ongoing renewal and regeneration of it. Therefore, growth in mature businesses often comes from mergers and acquisitions, and profit goes up because of savings, often following large layoffs. On the surface, companies may look to be successful and healthy even at times when their culture and capabilities are in decay. First generation management that had a passion for products and customers is substituted with a different type of manager that is more financially oriented. In the short term, this may result in higher growth and profits, but long-term sustained growth seldom comes from clever financial management. When finance enters the CEO's office, passion goes out.

Success always builds on one or more unique advantages for the company: a uniquely valuable or cost-effective product, a unique relation to or control over distribution, or some other factor that creates a type of temporary monopoly.

The company that has enjoyed such a monopoly for some time may make several mistakes without those mistakes having serious consequences. The monopoly has a built-in inertia as long as it continues to be a monopoly. But when the monopoly is lost, which may happen quickly, the consequences of past mistakes add up to rapid decline, which at this point is very difficult to stop. The apparent upward part of the corporate lifecycle therefore usually takes much longer than the downward part, the death cycle.

DEAFNESS

There are two main components in the ear that allow hearing:

1. The three bones that transmit sound from the tympanic membrane in the outer ear to the cochlea, which is the sensing organ in the inner ear.
2. The hair cells in the cochlea and the hearing center of the brain, which processes and interprets the sounds.

When the following happens, impairment occurs:

If the ear bones lose connection, the sound is not transmitted and the cochlea gets a poor signal. If hair cells break and the brain forgets its natural routine in interpreting what it hears, even a good signal is perceived as noise.

The organizational structure and the traditions are like the bones of the ear. If they don't function properly, management gets a poor signal. Culture and misperceptions of the reasons for success are like the brain. If they don't work properly, management misinterprets whatever signal it gets.

The process of being caught in the lifecycle is similar to the process of losing one's hearing: For many years, the hearing may actually deteriorate without the person noticing it. And when she actually realizes that she doesn't hear well any more, she most likely rejects the problem for a decade and blames others for not speaking clearly and loudly enough.

When people lose their hearing, an early stage reaction is to guess what was probably said and answer accordingly. Ask one question and answer another. And when the problem gets more serious, the hearing impaired will listen less and talk all the time.

Companies behave similarly. They think they know what the problem is and they act accordingly. Or they simply stop listening and do more of the things they know best.

Neither strategy works.

In addition, organizations seldom take responsibility for what happens. They tend to blame others for it: competition, currencies, customers, and globalization.

The resulting organizational deafness leads to a behavior that seems to be independent of industry and country:

- Organizations react more slowly to both problems and opportunities.

- Organizations tend to respond by doing more of the same rather than doing something different from what they are used to.

- Organizations maintain a self-perception of success long after success has gone away.

- Organizations reject ideas and solutions that were not invented within their organization's walls. They consider competitors and customers inferior to themselves. They know better.

- Organizations and their top management develop an increasingly arrogant approach to criticism. Long after they have lost the battle, they continue to act as if they own the world.

- Whatever may be left of entrepreneurial management is substituted by "professional" or financially based management, which believes that key financial figures are its most important tool to run the business.

- Focus shifts from long-term value creation to short-term bottom line. Downsizing, mergers, and acquisitions become the dominating responses to demands for better financial performance.

- The company team spirit changes into a culture of internal competition and friction. Ever more detailed internal accounting systems are introduced to improve financial accountability.

In short, innovation often goes out as financial management moves in. Examples are numerous. Exceptions are few. Think of some from your part of the world and answer the questions in the

Food for Thought section at the end of this chapter for each of them. You may also want to perform the more comprehensive self-assessment in Chapter 7, "The Toolbox."

THE FIRST CYCLE BECOMES A DEATH CYCLE

The first growth curve of a company may last from five to 50 years or sometimes even longer. Initial business model and product, marketing, or service concepts may be so unique that they last for generations with minor adjustments only. At least this was the situation 20 or 50 years ago.

At some point in time, the upward trend reverts. The question is not *whether* this turn occurs, but *when* it occurs. The downward trend is the second half of the first cycle—that is, the death cycle. It took Oticon about 10 years to lose everything the company had gained in the first 75 years of its lifetime. During this period of decay, both management and investors may well continue to perceive success: Downsizing improves short-term profits. Mergers or acquisitions may boost both top-line and bottom-line growth. Ambitious management goals may lift share prices and hit news headlines.

It is in this period of internal decay with increasingly short-term financially focused management that the company needs the second cycle the most. And it is probably also the time when the company most lacks the capability to create a second cycle.

This is not a new discovery, but it is a discovery that has become much more important. The reason is that change happens faster than before, and the nature of change is different: Companies don't primarily lose ground just because they are slow to adapt to a new situation. They lose because they don't realize that the new situation may be fundamentally new, thus requiring a fundamentally different approach instead of just a modified approach. They are so happy with their current mental model that they simply cannot imagine a radically different one.

Fundamentally, new situations occur more often than before because products and services contain much more knowledge than before—including new technologies and radically new materials. Moreover, buying habits move quickly—for example, from a specialized store to a hypermarket or from a physical store to the Internet.

Products as varied as eggs, cars, and banking services were once almost commodities. But now, you may buy eggs from different types of hens that have been fed and kept differently—for example, organically. Cars often come customized in every respect, and banks are no longer just banks.

Firms unable to anticipate or react very quickly to changing needs simply fall back. Hearing and reading the signs of the market has become ever more essential. Sticking to an outdated mental model can be fatal.

The choice is simple, but difficult to realize: You may either continue the first cycle downward or break it by fundamentally questioning its basis—that is, your mental model. If you dare do so, you have started to create the basis for your organization's second cycle.

FOOD FOR THOUGHT

Think of the current mental model of your organization:

- How does the company look upon customers, suppliers, employees, competitors, and the local community?

- What was the situation in which these views were formed?

- Which fundamental changes have occurred since these views were formed?

Do you want to analyze your organization's mental model further? Look at Chapter 7.

Here is a short checklist to help you determine whether your organization is about to get caught in the cycle:

- Does your organization anticipate or react to problems and opportunities as quickly today as it did when it was younger?

- When your organization faces a problem, does it consider responding in ways that are completely new to you?

- Are you aware of any competitor products, technologies, systems, or marketing concepts that are clearly superior to your organization's?

- Does your organization's current organic growth match the growth it had when it was younger?

- Will the CEO of your company think you are a great employee if you tell him or her that you honestly believe the company's business model is outdated?

- Judging from what your company actually *does*, is it more important that the company create long-term value than meet the budget?

- Are you and your fellow employees more empowered to make decisions than you were 10 years ago?

If you answered "no" to two or more of these questions, you should consider performing the self-assessment discussed in Chapter 7. You might be surprised!

2

The Second Cycle: A New Paradigm

THE DOWNWARD CYCLE

Many large, old, or successful organizations are already caught on the downward trend in their lifecycle. They may show nice financial figures due to downsizing or mergers and acquisitions, but behind the surface, they are slow-moving, they don't respond quickly and creatively to customer needs, and they are so happy with what they do that they spend all their time to refine it rather than to question it. In fact, if anybody questions their mental model, they get upset and immediately start defending themselves.

Such organizations are bound to die if they continue their current cycle. In the long run, no organization can win only through financial engineering and acquisitions if the organization is unable to meet customer needs and constantly innovate in all corners of the business. They will not experience a second cycle.

This chapter and the following four chapters provide you with a direction to look if you want to redesign your organization to create a second cycle—that is, to enable and sustain innovation and growth. The starting point is the change from conventional mass production (for example, a metal parts factory) to knowledge work (for example, investment banking) in general and customization and innovation in particular. It argues that the conventional hierarchical and functional organization is long overdue as an adequate structure for organizations that perform knowledge work. It highlights four fundamental characteristics of organizations that are essential if they want to exchange an upcoming death cycle with a second or a third lifecycle.

THE LINE-STAFF ORGANIZATION CANNOT DELIVER INNOVATION

The line-staff organization emerged about 100 years ago and was perfected in the U.S. automobile industry in the 1920s. It is related to the bureaucracy in government and public institutions, which was described and refined by German sociologist Max Weber in the end of the nineteenth century.

The core of the line-staff organization is a logical division of labor between employees that are specialists in each function of the company—for example, manufacturing, sales, and accounting. Within each so-called line function, there is a hierarchy, and the company management team is comprised of the top managers of each function. However, certain departments, such as personnel, are not related to one specific line function. These departments are staff functions. The organization works through interplay between line and staff functions, and the necessary coordination between functions takes place through contacts between functional managers, often through meetings.

If the organization produces identical items in identical boxes, nobody will be surprised to see that it looks like a machine, which is what the line-staff organization is. Each department has a well-defined function, each manager and each employee knows what to do, and the whole thing runs at a constant speed. The conventional line-staff organization is ideal for a manufacturing job, where constant high-quality output at the minimum cost is the name of game, particularly if the organization works in a relatively stable environment (see Table 2-1).

The strength of the functional and hierarchical organization is efficiency and stability. The more a job can be broken up in smaller parts, the more specialized each function becomes. Specialization also makes automization easier because each task is less complicated. However, the weakness is innovative capability.

Table 2-1 The Line-Staff Hierarchy Works Great for Manufacturing

What matters in a manufacturing organization?	Why the line-staff functional organization delivers that:
Constant, high-quality output	Clear functional responsibility for purchasing, inspection, planning, manufacturing, logistics, sales, and service.
Minimize training cost and maximize routine	Well-defined and constant jobs within a function. Formal procedures for ongoing monitoring of individual performance.
Ongoing cost reduction	Centralized engineering function in charge of ongoing rationalization effort. Ongoing monitoring of time usage and individual performance-based payment system. Specialized functions easier to automate and to outsource.
Maintain control over staff	Hierarchical management structure in which the manager has authority to organize work for each employee. Hire and fire and pay according to productivity.
Maximum capacity utilization	Two- or three-shift operation, seven days a week.

You might call such organizations *transaction based*. Their purpose is efficient delivery of transactions at a still lower cost and sufficiently high quality. However, manufacturing, or transaction-based, organizations tend to play a still less important role in established so-called industrialized societies compared to all the more creative functions, such as research and development (R&D), marketing and sales, customer service, and business development. Conventional manufacturing, or transaction-based, functions have moved to lower wage countries, primarily in Eastern Europe, Asia, and Latin America.

If innovation and customization are what matter, don't be surprised if the conventional machine organization (line-staff functional) just doesn't work. In fact, the conventional company as a whole won't be successful.

That's because innovation and customization are totally different jobs compared to stable, cost-efficient mass production. Table 2-2 outlines the main differences.

Table 2-2 Delivering Innovation Is a Different Ballgame from Mass Production

	Mass production	Innovation and mass customization
Output	Standardized, predictable.	Customized, unpredictable.
Primary criteria for success	Low cost, high quality, on-time delivery.	High value, high quality, highly customized, on-time delivery.
Workforce	Homogeneous, specialized, oriented primarily toward detail, low-risk, narrow focus.	Diverse, multi-skilled, oriented toward both whole and detail with a mix of risk-takers and security-oriented staff.
Need for learning and constant improvement	Avoid mistakes and waste, refine and constantly improve processes.	Understand customer needs, spot new trends and technologies, combine knowledge from different sources, and learn from customer experience.
Investments	Land, buildings, equipment, software, stock, training of employees.	People, research and development, IT systems, and training of employees individually and as project groups.
Communication key messages	Specifications, on-time deliveries, price.	Success stories, corporate values, and culture.

The organization that can deliver innovation and mass customization is not only slightly different from the conventional manufacturing business, it is a new paradigm. You may wonder why major corporations in all parts of the world have not yet realized that the conventional line-staff hierarchical organization just won't do the job in the knowledge economy. You may also wonder why highly paid management teams and boards of directors have not yet realized that they put their organizations at great risk by sticking to well-known hierarchical structures instead of designing new networked ones that are oriented toward the future instead of the past.

You may think that this applies primarily to conventional manufacturing industry and less to public institutions and private not-for-profit organizations. I don't believe so:

Think of a large not-for-profit organization, perhaps a charity, a youth organization, or a church:

- Will members or donors continue to be treated just as a number in a file and not as an important individual?

- Do you believe that organization will continue to be successful if it continues to do "more of the same" rather than innovating itself?

- In the future, do you think the organization will be like it is today, with no surprises and no unexpected competition?

There are several reasons why organizations—business, public, and others— tend to stick to old habits. Simple conservatism is probably the main reason. Many conventional line-staff organizations seem to do well even in today's rapidly changing environment. Don't fix it if it ain't broken! Another point is that the managers who rose to the top in the conventional organization probably will not be ideal for a different organizational setup. Rising to the top in a conventional organization takes muscle and power playing, whereas the open and transparent organization that I describe later in this chapter takes a different breed of leader. Few people will introduce an organizational model that makes them obsolete as managers. This is probably one of the most important reasons for the organizational conservatism that continues to prevail.

Organizational conservatism may also be because managers have not yet realized that the organizational setup is a key part of their mental model for doing business. The larger, the older, and the more successful the organization becomes, the more blinded it becomes in realizing that its current mental model may be outdated.

Most manufacturing organizations turn to lean manufacturing as the solution to an ever-increasing price pressure. Lean manufacturing is important, but for most businesses, it is not the essence. There will always be a cheaper place to produce. The essence is responsiveness, customization, and innovation. And the key to breaking the downward cycle is to design and run organizations that are highly efficient, responsive, and innovative.

That is not just a minor change. It is a new paradigm and indeed a new mental model for most conventional organizations.

Before we look upon that new mental model, consider some general observations on the shift from transaction-based to knowledge-based organizations.

WHY DO ORGANIZATIONS NEED TO BECOME KNOWLEDGE BASED?

One hundred years ago, when the conventional line-staff organization was designed, horses were still the most used means of transportation, telephones were for the few, education beyond seven years at school was rare, and almost all calculations were performed manually. Although many people felt that the world was changing rapidly, the pace of change was very slow in today's perspective. Knowledge was growing, and important discoveries were made, but compared to today, things were stable. Customers had very little choice compared with today, and products lived for decades with minor or no modifications in design and manufacturing methods.

The conventional line-staff organization was a clever answer to the question of how to best organize firms one hundred years ago. When firms got larger, there was no need to change the fundamental organizational concept; more departments could easily be added within the context of the existing overall structure.

Today, 100 years later, there are at least four fundamental reasons for the knowledge-based organization to gradually substitute transaction-based organizations:

- The *amount of available knowledge* has grown and continues to grow rapidly.

- Good quality products and services are available in virtually all fields, which eventually leads to competition on price for everybody that is not unique. Real advantages come from providing *innovative and radically different solutions*—yet at a competitive price.

- Customers or citizens look upon products and services in a still more *differentiated* fashion: Price-performance ratios are no longer the only criterion for purchase; environmental, emotional, ethical, and esthetical aspects play a greater role.

- As more and more knowledge is built into new products and services, *one-time costs* (such as R&D and marketing) become more important than unit manufacturing and transportation costs. Industries consolidate, and major suppliers are forced to serve global markets.

This list does not mean that knowledge-based organizations should focus less on efficiency. Cost is still an important factor in staying competitive, but it is no longer the most important factor.

 Before digging into the underlying reasons for this change, I suggest you take a look at your own organization:

- What are the three most important types of knowledge that determine the success of your organization? Do they come from the same source or from different sources?

- Comparing your organization with its colleagues or competitors, what is the most important reason for customers or members to choose your organization ahead of the others?

- Look at the costs to actually manufacture your product or deliver your service (the cost per unit) and compare those with the fixed costs, such as research and development, marketing, IT, and administration, divided by the volume you produce or deliver. Which type of cost (fixed or unit) has grown the fastest?

THE KNOWLEDGE EXPLOSION

Almost every industry has statistics that document that more knowledge and new products have been created in the last decade than in all the centuries before. This knowledge explosion offers a wide range of opportunities to not only improve product performance, but to revolutionize it.

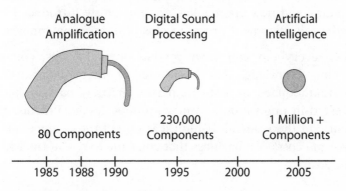

Figure 2-1 Hearing Aids Growth in Complexity

In the hearing aid business, for instance, the most advanced hearing aid in the world in 1988 had less than 100 electronic components, such as transistors, capacitors, and resistors. Seven years later, that figure had grown to about 230,000, and today, the computers that do the digital sound processing in hearing aids have millions of components (see Figure 2-1). More components doesn't necessarily make better hearing aids, but when the computer power of the hearing aid is used to host expert systems such as neural networks, the difference may be dramatic. Particularly, if the system is able to detect, separate, and amplify speech over noise according to the wish of the user. Knowledge comprises both the software and hardware technology of the chip and the psycho-acoustic knowledge about the brain's perception of speech and noise. Those competitors that did not have sufficient knowledge about both the technology and the use of it have already lost the game.

Often in industries, the most essential knowledge behind a breakthrough comes from outside the areas that were hitherto considered core competencies of the firm. CEO Niels Due Jensen of world leading water pump manufacturer Grundfos realized in the early 1990s that Grundfos was to get its lead through electronics that was completely foreign to the business. The potential for improvements in the hydraulic designs of the pumps has more of less been exhausted. After having exploited the potential of electronic controlled pumps, Grundfos now works with anthropologists to better understand the user interface of the pump and how errors may be avoided in the installation process. New knowledge domains and new approaches are constantly introduced into the product development process to foster continuous innovation.

When everybody can move production to low-cost countries, it becomes knowledge that determines whether a company wins at the marketplace or not—in particular, that part of knowledge invested in innovation and new product design. Product development and the research behind it is one of the components in the one-time costs of a business that continue to rise at the expense of unit costs.

ONE-TIME COSTS DOMINATE UNIT COSTS

The amount of knowledge put into new products and services has led to a steep increase in one-time costs for research and development and marketing as opposed to unit costs for manufacturing and distribution. Some industries have seen one-time costs go up by a factor of 5 or 10 over a decade, whereas manufacturing costs have remained stable or even dropped by 25 percent or more, in real terms (see Table 2-3).

Table 2-3 Most One-Time Costs Grow, While Most Unit Costs Decline

	One-time costs	Unit costs
Growing cost elements	Develop and acquire knowledge, combine knowledge from different sources, convert knowledge to products and services, test and document value to customers, and develop and implement marketing and sales activities.	Quality assurance.
Declining cost elements	Communication costs.	Manufacturing, logistics (inbound and outbound).
Overall effect	Growing, probably doubled over the last five years.	Declining.

As one-time costs become dominant, it becomes relatively more attractive to sell one's product globally. After all, the high one-time costs have already been spent and the marginal cost of manufacturing and distributing extra units is small. This becomes fatal for small competitors that do not have the resources or the knowledge to develop still more advanced and more expensive new product generations sufficiently fast. Price becomes their only weapon, and in the end, they are bound to lose.

Globalization prevails.

INNOVATION IS THE ESSENCE

Why did IBM miss the PC game? Why did Sears miss the hypermarket opportunity? Why did Boeing miss the mid-range passenger aircraft business? Why did Germany miss the manufacturing revolution?

Each company or government offers its own explanation, but to me, it looks like there is one reason that is more important than all the others: lack of innovative capability.

IBM, Sears, Boeing, and Germany were obsessed with improving their current mental models. Management was directed by bonuses based on short-term financial performance. Although they celebrated their respective successes, Dell, Wal-Mart, Airbus, and Ireland saw new opportunities and went for them.

A small company called Unimerco, for example, is in one of the most boring businesses you can imagine: maintaining (sharpening) metal tools for manufacturers in the wood and metal sectors in Europe and the U.S. Twenty years ago, it was nothing to be proud of. It was just another local business-to-business (B2B) service business competing primarily on price in a market that had already shown signs of decline due to outsourcing of manufacturing to Asia and Latin America.

Unimerco could have chosen to move into other businesses, something more in touch with the times. But Unimerco's CEO Kenneth Iversen chose a different path: Why not put together a package that we know no one else offers—a unique combination of product, service, and relationship that could enhance the overall productivity of customers' manufacturing operations that would not be immediately outsourced to low-cost countries?

Built around its core expertise, Unimerco designed a package that would effectively allow manufacturing industries to outsource their tool management operations to Unimerco with significant gains in productivity as a result. Unimerco had the capability to change: Management and staff owned the majority of the company, and the majority of staff members were also shareholders. No tough arguments with unions about the change. No resistance. Just go for it.

Unimerco gained world leadership in its field within the next two decades. Its customer list now includes Airbus, Boeing, BMW, Ford, and General Motors. Recently, Unimerco has taken the step to not only help manufacturing businesses in European and the U.S. become more productive, it has established itself in China and plans to cover Eastern Europe and Latin American manufacturing operations within three years.

Innovation is the essence. No conventional hierarchical organization could achieve what Unimerco has done. At Unimerco, management, sales, and administrative staff have no offices. They sit in the very production environment, next to and in between machines. Communication is open and direct. Issues are raised and dealt with immediately. Networks have substituted hierarchy. The collaborative vision has become reality. Unimerco got out of the lifecycle trap.

It might seem as if industries, countries, and individual companies differ so much that there is no common pattern behind. But there is.

A NEW PARADIGM: THE COLLABORATIVE ORGANIZATION

There are four basic, common aspects for organizations that can continuously adapt to changing environments and continuously apply knowledge in new ways to create innovations in products, processes, and services:

- They have a *meaning*, which goes beyond that of making a profit or being the industry leader.
- They involve a fundamental *partnership* between management and staff, and they do not look upon the two as opposites. The partnership also extends to suppliers, customers, and other partners outside of the organization.
- They are organized for *collaboration*—that is, less structured and more organic and chaotic than a conventional business.
- They are led by people who base their jobs on *shared values* rather than authority and power.

We need a term to describe that new paradigm organization. I suggest we call it a *collaborative organization*. The first time I created such an organization was in 1991 at troubled hearing aid manufacturer Oticon. At that time, we called it the spaghetti organization. Spaghetti sounds a little crazy at first, but the metaphor is quite precise: Think of a pot with well-boiled spaghetti, the long thin stuff, which the Italians call *tagliarini* or *capelli di angelo*. It looks like every part of this material is connected to everything else. There is no hierarchy. There are no barriers. It is one big system and a lot of small organisms at the same time. That's what the organization of the future will be like.

The four key characteristics of the collaborative organization compared to the classical line-staff model are shown in Table 2-4.

Table 2-4 Line-Staff Versus Collaborative

	The Old Paradigm: Line-Staff	The New Paradigm: Collaborative
Meaning	Maximize financial return to shareholders.	Contribute to a multitude of relevant stakeholders.
Relation to staff and to the outside world	Employees are opposites. Buy-sell relationships between external parties such as suppliers and customers.	Employees are partners in the business. Interdependent "win-win" network relationships with external parties.
Organization	Highly organized and departmentalized line-staff organization.	Apparently disorganized "spaghetti" structure based on highly refined business processes.
Basis for management	Authority and power.	A psychological contract based on shared values and norms.

In the following chapters, you will explore each of these four aspects one by one. They will not guarantee you a successful second cycle, but they all add to the likelihood that your organization will be able to create one. They are not independent. For example, if your organization has implemented a collaborative organization without having established an overall meaning to all employees, the flexible organization will most likely not work in a coordinated manner. Likewise, if you have done all the rest but still treat your employees like opposites rather than associates, you will probably experience that the employees will misuse their newly granted freedom.

The four elements of the new paradigm all represent continuous action rather than a one-time effort. You cannot vaccinate your organization against the negative aspects of success, but you may be able to prevent them from taking over by making the four points a daily fitness program.

Although the elements of the fitness program make sense for almost any organization, the way the program should be implemented varies by industry, region, organization type, and size. One size doesn't necessarily fit all. My experience indicates the following:

- *Meaning* is particularly important for organizations that employ people that need to think about what they are doing and why—that is, the opposite of the assembly line worker that might as well be substituted by a robot.

- *Partnership* is important for all organizations. Managing organizations through fear and power won't work long term anywhere. The alternatives for employees, customers, and suppliers are just too many.

- *Collaboration* is essential for organizations that need to customize their offering, to differentiate themselves from competition, and to move fast.

- *Leadership* based on values instead of just figures is most needed for organizations in transition. In a stable environment, doing the same thing as last year, just a little bit better or faster, will be sufficient in many cases. But few environments are stable any more.

FOOD FOR THOUGHT

Think of your organization today in light of the transformation of business from "transaction-based" toward "knowledge-based":

- Which parts of your organization are mostly transaction-based and which parts are mostly knowledge-based?

- Which parts have been growing or declining over the past 10 years?

- Is your organizational structure radically different or similar in the transaction-based and the knowledge-based parts of the business?

- When was your organization fundamentally designed? Has the amount and variety of knowledge that you apply changed since the organization was designed?

- Does the design of your organization more or less look like that of your main competitors?
- What is your organization's meaning? How would you describe the relationship between management and staff? Do you see your suppliers as partners? Is your organizational structure rigid or organic? Do you lead through budgets or through values?

3

Meaning

FOCUS ON MEANING RATHER THAN ACTIVITY

You have no doubt many times thought about the foundation for your organization—that is, the very meaning of it. Many companies claim that the core is their unique technology or their unique high performance products. Some claim it is the relation they have to their unique customers or their loyal and competent employees. It probably isn't.

Think of a mobile phone company such as Nokia. The key technology is in the chips that process data, transfer data to the network, and make the whole thing work for you. Plus, there is the software, the battery, and maybe the antenna design.

Few customers actually buy that. They buy product. They look for features such as innovative design, small size, good battery lifetime, speech quality, photo and video capabilities, user interface, and the like.

However, the product in itself is not worth much as a standalone piece of hardware. Imagine if you were the only person in the world who owned a mobile phone. It wouldn't be worth much for you. The product is only of value because it attaches to the mobile networks. So the network is the solution, which makes the product valuable for you.

Why do you want that particular solution? Not because you are fascinated by chips, batteries, software, or antennas. Not because you are thrilled with the product design and features. Not because you are impressed with the network. You fundamentally want the mobile phone because you want to be connected. "Connecting people" is Nokia's motto. I believe this is the best possible motto for a mobile phone manufacturer because it reflects the very meaning of mobile telephony and therefore the very meaning of Nokia as a company.

Table 3-1 looks at the four foundations that give meaning to a company: its technology, the products that build on it, the solution that makes it work, and the meaning, which is why you want the product.

Table 3-1 The Foundations of Organizational Meaning

	Definition	Example: Mobile telephony
Meaning	What makes the product attractive	Connecting people
Solution	What makes the product work	The network
Product	What makes the product real	Mobile phone
Technology	What makes the product possible	Chips, software, battery, antenna

The four foundations are important aspects of the company, but only the first one actually gives meaning to the business. Technology, product design, and the particular network solution may change, but Nokia as a company does not fundamentally change because the meaning has not changed. For Nokia, the three other foundations may be changed as new opportunities arrise. It may one day decide to leave the mobile telephony business. But as long as Nokia is in this business, the meaning will stand: connecting people.

Meaning is not a term that appears frequently in business discussions and textbooks. Normally, we speak about *mission* (what the company strives to be), *vision* (where the company intends to go), and *strategy* (how the company will get there). We talk about the *value proposition* to customers (what it will do for the customer), but not about meaning. Meaning expresses *why* the company exists—that is, why it would be fundamentally missed if it did not exist.

Think of a company in an industry you know. Identify its key technologies, its products, the solutions, and the meaning of that business. Look at its website. You will be surprised how many companies focus on their technologies and their products rather than the meaning of the whole thing.

Table 3-2 shows other examples.

Table 3-2 Meaning in Four Industries

Industry	Mobile telephones	Tool maintenance	Hearing aids	Cleaning
Meaning	Connecting people.	Productivity improvement.	Better quality of life for people with impaired hearing.	Attractive and healthy work environment, which improves business competitiveness.
Solution	The network.	Efficient delivery and tool management system.	Equipment and trained staff to analyze hearing and fit the instrument to the needs of the user.	Analyzing demand, choosing cleaning methods and levels, delivering consistent service.
Product	Mobile phone.	Sharpening.	Hearing aid.	Cleaning.
Technology	Chips, software, battery, antenna.	Machinery for grinding, cutting, polishing, and so on.	Signal processing chips and software, transducers, moulding technology.	Chemicals, equipment, procedures, and systems for cleaning.

In many industries (including the examples in Table 3-2), companies tend to forget the meaning and focus on the underlying activities:

- Most tool maintenance companies focus on sharpening tools rather than helping their customers achieve higher productivity or higher product quality through the use of the right tools for the jobs they have.

- Most hearing aid manufacturers focus on their products and their technology while forgetting what really matters: how to make people that use their hearing aids smile.

- Cleaning companies feature their unique equipment and their highly trained staff instead of focusing on the appearance and healthiness of the customer's working environment, which is the only thing that really matters to their customers.

MEANING APPLIES TO ALL TYPES OF ORGANIZATIONS

You might think that discovering meaning is only a matter for private enterprise. It is not.

Take a public school, for example. The *technology* is its buildings, A/V equipment, and the carefully thought-out curriculum. The *product* is teaching. The *solution* is everything done to manage students and interact with their parents. But the *meaning* is personal growth of each individual student into a responsible and capable adult, who is ready for further studies, for work, and for life.

Is personal growth for each individual student what your local school focuses on? Perhaps it seems like that when you listen to the school's principal during the graduation speech. But in the day-to-day operation, it seldom is. Buildings, teachers, curriculum, and finances matter more.

As another example, take Scouting.[1] Scouting is the world's largest voluntary youth movement with about 35 million members worldwide. You see scouts on the streets in uniforms, you see them helping at disasters, and you see them performing a variety of activities in your local community. The "technology" behind Scouting is its youth program design, which guides young people through a progressive scheme of activities. Also, the concept of volunteer leaders supported by training and program material is part of Scouting's technology. What you see is the "product"—that is, the actual activities in your local community or elsewhere. The scout uniform is part of the product. However, the product is part of a

---

[1] Scouting is used as a common denominator for both the World Organization of the Scout Movement and the World Association of Girl Guides and Girl Scouts.

larger "solution," which includes the interaction with parents and different institutions in the local community; but none of this is the true meaning of Scouting. The meaning is to stimulate the physical, intellectual, social, emotional, and spiritual development of young people—that is, to allow young people to realize their full potential.

As a volunteer organization, Scouting has no power to force its leaders to do the job. If leaders do not do their job properly, the only thing Scouting can do is ask them to leave. Therefore, Scouting needs to constantly focus on the meaning of the organization in order to maintain unity and focus in the organization. If Scouting forgets this focus and sticks to technology or product, it will soon become outdated. Activities need to constantly change, uniforms must be modified, and organizational structures must be adapted to changing needs. But the meaning stands.

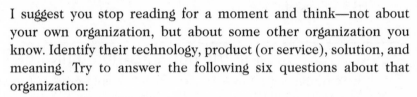 I suggest you stop reading for a moment and think—not about your own organization, but about some other organization you know. Identify their technology, product (or service), solution, and meaning. Try to answer the following six questions about that organization:

1. Is the meaning, as you identified it, the essence of the organization's communication to customers or members?

2. Does the day-to-day behavior of management clearly reflect the meaning?

3. Is there anything the organization does significantly different from competitors that you can track directly back to the particular meaning of the organization?

4. Is there a clear connection between the meaning of the organization and the way it expresses its mission, vision, strategy, and values?

5. If you buy a product or a service from the organization, does the product, the service, or the way it is delivered remind you or alert you to the meaning of the organization?

6. Does the meaning play any important role in the way the organization attracts and hires people for employment or voluntary work?

After you answer these six questions, go back and look upon the number of no's. If there are more than two no's, I dare say that the organization is more focused on technology, product, and solution rather than meaning. I would invest my money or time elsewhere.

MEANING IS THE KEY

Meaning is the key to all the rest: If a company is to become a true partnership with the customer, there needs to be a meaning behind its actions. You need a common cause that all participants can adhere to. You need a common direction to guide the cooperation between different parts of the organization and those outside the organization that need to contribute. You need meaning to allow staff to work not in departments, but in spaghetti organizations. And, you certainly need meaning to serve as the basis for the values of the organization.

THE ACID TEST: WHAT IF THE ORGANIZATION DIDN'T EXIST?

If Scouting ceased to exist, few people would miss it if it was just a collection of leisure time activities carried out by volunteer leaders with kids in uniform in the local community. However, because Scouting is an educational system that aims at the development of young people to realize their full potential and take a constructive place in society, it would be greatly missed if it didn't exist. It is the meaning that makes the difference.

If the public school model was only a delivery system for passing knowledge and skills to young people, it would be easy to substitute with something else if it didn't exist. But if it has meaning in the sense that it successfully helps young people grow into responsible and capable adults, it would be greatly missed if it didn't exist.

If tool maintenance company Unimerco ceased to exist, tools could be sharpened elsewhere. But the productivity of its clients would suffer because Unimerco focuses on customer productivity rather than sharpening tools. Whether a tool is 100 percent sharp is a limited part of overall productivity. Therefore, Unimerco takes a broader look. Unimerco would be greatly missed by manufacturing companies if it ceased to exist.

If an ordinary cleaning company went out of business, there would be 10 other cleaning companies offering the same service to customers. Nobody would notice. But if a cleaning company that had made a major difference for workplace appearance and health went away, it would be greatly missed, simply because workplace appearance and health is the meaning of cleaning.

 Ask yourself: What would society miss if your company or organization didn't exist any more? Of course, employees, their families, and the local community would suffer. But who else? That's the acid test for determining the meaning of your company.

PERFORM THE OBITUARY TEST

In his book *Storytelling—Branding in Practice*, Klaus Fog proposes the ultimate test on meaning for an organization: the obituary test. He proposes that you write down your company's obituary as follows:

- How would the obituary read if your customers were to write it?
- How would the obituary read if your competitors were to write it?
- What would the world look like if your company did not exist?
- If your company would close tomorrow, who would miss it?
- Has your company made any real difference to your stakeholders?

Most companies would not be missed by anyone other than their owners and the employees. Most of them make very little difference. Most of them lack meaning.

MEANING MUST PENETRATE EVERY ASPECT OF THE BUSINESS

The key point is that all organizations, public and private, should go through a process in which they discover their meaning. They should understand clearly what would be missed if the organization suddenly ceased to exist. That's the easy part. The difficult part is to review every corner of the business in light of the meaning. Unimerco would ask itself: Does this activity help improve our customers' productivity? Scouting would ask: Does this help young people realize their full potential, physically, intellectually, socially, emotionally, and spiritually? And the cleaning company would check how every single activity, department, or employee contributes to workplace appearance and health.

In many companies, departments, reports, meetings, activities, expenses, procedures, and habits don't really contribute to the meaning of the company. They don't add genuine value to customers. The consequence should be clear: They should be discontinued unless they were absolutely necessary for other reasons, such as proper bookkeeping or meeting relevant legal requirements.

The savings that follow from this process can be impressive, but that's the least important part. The essence of the process is the focus it brings to everything that the company *continues* to do.

Look at a conventional hospital, for example. As a patient, you enter into a system that was never designed with you in mind. It is a health factory designed for maximum efficiency from the doctor's point of view. You are asked the same questions over and over again. You meet one doctor today and another tomorrow. You wait and wait and wait until finally it is your turn to have a certain examination or test. What is the meaning? Optimizing the working conditions for doctors and other health personnel? The meaning is to help you get better as quickly as possible so you can regain the quality of life you lost somehow by falling ill. Few hospitals are focused on that, and few hospitals are benchmarked on that. Hospitals are benchmarked on efficiency and treatment outcome, not on patient satisfaction. A hospital that focused on patients rather than on doctors and administration would be greatly missed if it didn't exist.

MEANING AND THE MENTAL MODEL

Meaning is an essential part of the mental model of an organization, perhaps the one part that is the most difficult to change.

If a manufacturer of medical instrumentation has spent the last 50 years refining its instruments for hospital laboratory use, it has most likely perfected instrument precision, throughput, cost per test, and interface to other laboratory systems. The mission statement of the business is probably to provide high-precision information for doctors in a hospital setting. The sales force most likely is highly professional and trained in calling laboratory managers and hospital purchasing agents. Marketing focuses on the conferences and exhibitions that laboratory managers attend and the media they read. Logistics and services have been designed to attend to the needs of relatively few laboratories.

When technology allows tests to be performed by the general practitioner, the medical instrumentation company will most likely develop a smaller and less expensive instrument for general practitioner (GP) use.

However, changing the product is only a minor part of the change. It also needs to change its distribution, service, sales, and marketing in order to move from the hospital laboratory to the GP's office.

The meaning and the entire mental model in general must be changed. GPs don't really need ultimate precision instruments. They go for whatever help they can get to diagnose and treat their patients quicker, less expensively, and with less hassle. They will judge the instrument on hassle-free operation, easy-to-understand results, and whatever help they can get in passing on the benefits to their patients.

Such change of meaning and mental model is very difficult for a precision medical instrumentation company. However, this change is the prerequisite for success as the market place changes. The difficulty to change meaning and mental model in general increases with company size and success rate. The larger and the more successful a company becomes, the more obsessed it will be with its current mental model. Employees who discover the need for change are encouraged not to put their concerns forward. Managers do not reward people who challenge the basis for their jobs.

If you run a railroad service, a hearing aid company, a cleaning business, a community service, an instrument business, a pump business, or maybe a vegetable farm, you have to decide what the meaning of the business is. Normally, there is more than one possible meaning. The hearing aid company, for example, could either focus on helping adults with moderate hearing loss achieve higher quality of life or it could help children with severe hearing loss gain some ability to hear. Having defined the meaning, you align everything the company does to serve that purpose. On the contrary, if you run the railroad because you are obsessed with trains, customers will most likely go elsewhere. Your company will continue on the downward cycle and there will not be a second cycle at all.

Table 3-3 lists five examples of companies and the meaning (and lack of meaning) they might assign themselves.

Table 3-3 Five Examples of Meaning (and Lack of Meaning) in Different Industries

Type of product or service provided	What's the meaning—and what's not?
Railroad transport	The meaning is *not* just to get something or someone from A to B cheaply and efficiently. Many different means of transport can do that. The meaning is to do it *safer* than any other means of transport. Or more *environmentally friendly*. Or *faster*. Or *more comfortably*. Whatever is a real need for customers and at the same time possible to achieve.
Service for the elderly	The meaning is *not* just to provide four hours of practical assistance per week to every pensioner in the neighborhood. Everybody can do that. The meaning could be to improve his quality of life, to help keep him self-sufficient, and keep him attached to family and friends.
Scientific instrument used in healthcare industry	The meaning of this is *not* to provide doctors with ever more precise measuring data. The meaning could be to help doctors save more patient's lives within specific fields or help them save time so that they can serve more patients every day. It is what the doctor does with the instrument and with the results that matter.
Home circulation pump	The meaning is *not* just to move hot water efficiently in the house. Any circulator can do that. The meaning could be to circulate hot water with higher comfort (that is, with less noise), lower energy need, or longer lifetime (that is, no repairs, no hassle).
Vegetable farm	The meaning is *not* just to produce vegetables efficiently. Many companies do that. The meaning could be to produce vegetables that simply taste better. Or perhaps are easier to prepare. Or maybe vegetables that are completely free for pollution of any kind.

There is a pattern emerging: The meaning is the essence of what makes the product valuable for customers.

WHY IS MEANING ESSENTIAL FOR THE CREATION OF A SECOND CYCLE?

The laziness, complacency, and arrogance that develop in the late stages of the first cycle and eventually lead to decline and death can be counteracted with concrete measures such as a reduction of management layers, more open communication, new workplace design, and more involvement of employees and suppliers in the business as partners instead of opposites. Although some of these measures may have a positive effect, they will most likely not create a second cycle if there is not a meaning behind the whole thing that goes beyond just making a profit. The meaning serves several functions:

- The meaning is the *overall guideline* for everything the company does. Unless the medical instrumentation company really helps doctors do a better job with their patients, the rest doesn't matter: design, cost-efficiency, precision, features, and smart marketing campaigns. Therefore, the meaning is the common direction for management, employees, and external partners.

- The meaning determines the *direction of innovation* in product design, supply chain design, processes, marketing, sales, and service. Every innovation must somehow contribute to realizing the meaning better or less expensively.

- The meaning is the turning point for all *internal and external communication*. Every change or every new product or service must be communicated within the context of the overall meaning of the company.

- The meaning ultimately determines the *relevance of organizational and other changes* within the company and its partner network, in particular, its supply chain. If a change does not move the organization toward better or more efficiently delivering its meaning, it is worthless.

Meaning is an overall concept that encompasses the positioning of the organization, its identity, and its value propositions toward main stakeholders. Several competitors in one industry may go for the same meaning, but such competitors often develop very differently. It may be hard to phrase the meaning of the organization precisely, but the hard part is to make sure it penetrates everything the organization does.

In Chapter 7, "The Toolbox," you will find a Mental Model Mapper to help you find the meaning of your organization and to build it into your mental model. You will also find a tool that helps you create consensus among all employees and managers in your organization about the meaning and the values you have chosen to base your work on.

FOOD FOR THOUGHT

- What would your customers miss if your organization didn't exist?

- Would there be protests from customers if you went out of business or would they be able to find an alternative supplier easily? If yes, what would the protests be about?

- Would competitors be able to easily fill the vacuum after your business left the market?

- Why is it that your customers want your product or competition's product? What is the benefit they get out of that product? Why is the benefit important for them?

- What would a "dream product" look like from the customer's point of view?

- What would the product have to do or look like in order to be worth twice today's price for your customers?

- Sharpen your ability to spot the meaning of an organization. Pick a voluntary association that you belong to. What is its meaning and what would its obituary look like?

4

Partnership

OPPOSITES OR PARTNERS?

Internally and externally, the second pillar of the new platform for second cycle growth is partnership. In this chapter, I use two different words for partnership: In relation to employees, I talk about *partnership*; whereas, in dealing with suppliers and other external partners, I use the term *networking* to express relationships between the organization and other parties that have been designed to support "win-win" relationships.

Think of a company or some other organization. Look at its annual report. Look for its values. In most cases, you will find nothing. On the surface, it looks like most organizations do well without values that are written down. However, that is only what it looks like on the surface. Every organization is built on values. The most important values are how the organization looks upon its customers (or members or citizens) and suppliers, and how it views its employees.

Among those companies that publish their values, a frequent phrase reads, "Our employees are our most important asset." Although you may question whether it makes

sense to compare human beings with assets such as buildings and
equipment, the meaning is that the company values the skills,
knowledge, and attitudes of their employees. So far, so good.

The problem is that those phrases are often pure varnish. Reality
may be completely different: Companies hire and fire according to
short-term demand, while maintaining that their employees are their
most important asset. Companies introduce ever more detailed and
rigorous control systems, while maintaining that they have full confidence in their employees. Companies and labor unions go through
long-lasting and confrontational bargaining processes and strikes.
Both parties talk about the company as one big family.

Most managers quite simply have a mental model that assumes
that the company and the employees are opposites. It need not be
that way. A company and its employees can be partners. Actually,
the two must be partners if they want to build organizations that
break the death cycle—that is, achieve sustainable success.

TWO DIFFERENT MENTAL MODELS

The difference between the two different mental models, opposites
or partners, covers much more than the formal relationship, as
illustrated in Table 4-1.

Table 4-1 Comparing Two Mental Models

	Opposites	Partners
Underlying value	Staff is a production factor that can be purchased at market price. The relation is primarily legal and buy-sell.	Staff is an essential part of the company, which is attached to the organization through a human and emotional relationship rather than just a legal one.
Role of management	Management analyzes, decides, organizes, implements, controls, and rewards. Rewards are linked to quantitative goals.	Management interacts with staff, involves staff in all issues, sets overall direction and framework, establishes milestones, gains commitment, monitors progress, and celebrates achievements with staff.
Role of employees	Employees do the work as ordered. They work according to agreements and rules, often collectively agreed. Most work is well defined and individual. Co-operation with others takes place mostly within formal meetings.	Staff members participate extensively in planning and decision-making processes and are involved in setting their own goals. They interact freely and informally with others, inside and outside the organization.

	Opposites	Partners
Physical workplace	Management sits in offices that are separated from ordinary staff. Executive assistants serve management to save time and protect management from unwanted visitors.	Management works physically among staff and rarely has offices. Executive assistants ensure that management is available for dialog with staff members and others.
Ownership	Employees are a production factor that has no ownership to the organization.	Employees are natural co-owners of the organization and have a say at board level as employee-elected board members or as shareholders. Employees behave like owners.
Termination	Employees that are not essential to the organization can be laid off if they are no longer necessary.	Staff members are rarely terminated. In case of a drop in business volume, the company strives to find solutions that allow staff to stay as long as possible.

The key point is the underlying value or mental model: Do you consider staff a production factor like raw materials or electricity, or is the staff an essential part of the company?

EIGHT TOUGH QUESTIONS

If you are a manager, take five minutes to perform a self-test by answering the eight questions that follow:

1. When an employee leaves after 10 years in your company, would you in most cases consider his exit a normal event that does not prompt you to be concerned?

2. If business gets tough and your budgeted profit gets under pressure, would you normally consider layoffs as a means to restore profitability?

3. If an employee does an excellent job and demands twice the industry average salary, would you normally argue that such great difference in pay is not your company's policy?

4. The last time you reviewed your company's mission statement, did you involve only management and the board of directors (no employees)?

5. If your company runs into a serious problem, would you normally try to sort it out in the management group without telling your employees?

6. Do you consider labor unions (if they are present in your company) as opposites that you need to manage in a way that minimizes their influence?

7. If an employee wants to speak with you, does she need to go through an executive assistant or secretary to get an appointment?

8. If you could decide to expand the present shareholder group of your company with employees, would you recommend that extended ownership of your company was limited to directors and other senior staff members only?

If you answer yes to two or more of these questions, you should seriously consider your mental model concerning employees. You may think that you are very "people oriented" (most managers do), but are you sure that you practice what you preach?

Look at some of the questions again if you answered yes:

- *Leaving after 10 years.* If employees leave after 10 years, they should have built up tremendous knowledge about the industry, your business, customers, products, supply chain, and more. If the employee was good, the company loses great amounts of knowledge, which should not be considered a normal part of business. If the employee was not good, he should not have stayed with you for so long. Keeping an employee for 10 years that doesn't fill his or her job definitely should not be a part of normal business.

- *Twice the industry average salary.* An excellent employee is probably not only twice as good as the industry average, but rather 10 or 20 times better. Doubling salary from industry average is still an excellent deal for the company. Aren't you attracting average people by paying average salaries?

- *Sorting out problems in the management team.* First of all, don't think you can hide a serious problem. Everyone in your organization will know about it. And why not involve all the brains in the organization in dealing with a problem and solving it?

- *Employee ownership.* If you and your management team think it is attractive to become co-owners, your employees will most likely also think so. If you think it turns out to become a good deal for you, it will also become a good deal for them. If you are motivated to gain the up side and avoid the down side, why would your employees think differently?

You most likely need to consider your mental model about employees very seriously. If you continue to view them as opposites, they will view you and your company as an opposite. Can you create a winning organization that way?

EVERYBODY NEEDS TO THINK—NOT ONLY MANAGEMENT

My thinking may be influenced by the Scandinavian tradition where there is little distance and difference between managers and employees. But the need to make employees become partners is not restricted to Scandinavia. It is a global trend.

International comparisons of competitive power or business climate consistently rank the Nordic countries (Denmark, Finland, Iceland, Norway, and Sweden) on top of the lists when it comes to flexibility and motivation of workforce.

The reason is that innovative and responsive organizations cannot be managed by detailed analysis, planning, and control. Every single employee needs to be involved in analysis, planning, control, learning, and innovation. The routine jobs have been outsourced or automated. What's left is the knowledge and innovation-intensive tasks such as interaction with customers, research, development, marketing, sales, service, planning, and management.

These functions require *everyone* to think, work together across borders, and be creative—not only the management. It is this type of work that cannot be managed by detailed analysis, planning, and control. It takes employees that are motivated, creative, flexible, mobile, and involved. Moreover, much work can be done or needs to be done outside of the office, often in the home. Therefore, management must give up conventional control and learn new types of motivation and followup.

A NEW RELATIONSHIP

The shift from opposites to partners requires a new mental model for both management and staff.

Managers need to do the following:

- Interact more informally and more intensively with staff, working together rather than issuing orders and controlling performance.

- Move out of their protected offices and work directly with the staff. Managers must be constantly available for consultation and discussion.

- Understand the three different aspects of management:

   Drive for results.

   Ensure professional quality.

   Provide the framework for every single employe to do her best (the mentor role) and to constantly develop as a professional and as a human being.

- Reward employees in a way that reflects their contribution to the company in a broad sense rather than objective criteria such as formal education and seniority.

In other words, managers must not only look upon themselves as captains of the ship; they are also *naval architects* that design the ship and redesign it while sailing as conditions change. Redesigning an organization is much more than structure and the physical environment. It starts with the fundamental human values that determine what the organization does every day. You can read more about defining values and leading through values in Chapter 6, "Leadership," and Chapter 7, "The Toolbox."

On the other side of the relationship, employees also have to embark upon a different mental model. Employees need to do the following:

- Accept that they are in the same boat as the company; they must do everything they reasonably can to contribute to make the company successful.

- Make an effort to understand not only their own job, but also the interplay between their work and other people's work.

- Involve themselves more actively in the issues of the company. Employees need not only do what they are told, but they should actively seek opportunities and solutions to problems.

- Interact more closely and more frequently with managers and employees from other departments.

- Become more flexible and be willing to make an extra effort when needed.

Creating value in an organization is done neither by management nor by employees alone. Management and employees create value together. If they consider themselves opposites, they may still be able to create value; but if they want to create great value and have fun, there needs to be a true teamwork based on a common goal.

In many companies, more and more functions get outsourced to subsuppliers or freelancers—that is, providers of service functions that are not part of the organization's core business. The main advantage is that outsiders may concentrate on their business while the company concentrates on its core business.

Such freelancers should be treated like associates. Their contribution to the company is equally valuable, and there is an equal need for them to take ownership of the company's success.

THE WORKPLACE: BARRIER OR BRIDGE?

The physical workplace is often a barrier for the more informal and intense relationship between management and employees. Managers need to give up the privileges of corner offices and executive assistants that protect them from unwanted interaction with staff. An open door isn't enough when the manager signals that she really isn't interested in interaction. Managers need to be available for consultation and interaction during the entire workday. Managers should work in open spaces in direct contact with employees. It goes without saying that managers and employees both need places of privacy. Such rooms should be available for everyone to book on a short-term basis—that is, not permanently.

CO-OWNERSHIP IF POSSIBLE

An essential part of the partnership thinking is sharing the ups and downs of the business. It is ideal if staff can be invited to buy shares in the business. There are several employee share schemes in which employees are invited to make an investment at a discount. Even at a discount, a real cash investment is far superior to warrants or stock options. When the employee is faced with the decision to sacrifice cash in order to make an investment, he is forced to decide if he believes in the company or not. If the employee decides in favor of investing, he will have a much higher commitment to the company than employees that have been granted stock options. Even a few thousand dollars make a tremendous psychological difference. If the scheme is repeated year after year at prices corresponding—for example, to the book value per share minus a discount—employees may end up having made significant investments, which add up to a strong commitment to the company.

Critics claim that such investments increase the risk of the employees. In bad times, they risk being laid off and suffering a loss on their shares. But the advantages of having everyone in the same boat financially makes such situations much less likely. The loss on shares can also be limited if the net offering price is less than book value at the time of purchase—for example, a 50 percent discount.

World-leading tool management company Unimerco has an interesting employee ownership scheme that has brought consistent growth in revenues and profits over decades in an industry that is highly uncertain due to rapid development of new technologies and the relocation of manufacturing units of Unimerco key customers from Western Europe and the U.S. to low-wage countries in Eastern and central Europe, Asia, and Latin America. The essence is that employees borrow money to invest in the business, thus sharing the risk of doing business with everyone else. The value of shares is linked to performance according to a formula, which is well-known and understood by all employees. The company has opted out of layoffs as a means to restore profitability in case of financial trouble. Everyone simply works harder until the issue has been resolved.

THE ACID TEST: AVOID HIRE-AND-FIRE

When times get tough, management has a unique opportunity to prove if it really means that the relationship between employees and the company is a partnership. It is not fair to expect a company to sit down and do nothing in the case of a severe drop in sales. If maintaining all staff puts the company in severe trouble, it will be better to maintain some staff and save the company. However, there is much that the company can do to avoid firing staff:

- Salaries can be reduced on a voluntary basis either proportionally or at percentages that are higher for higher paid staff and management.

- Working hours can be reduced temporarily to match the lack of sales volume.

- Outsourced functions can be insourced to create employment for persons who would otherwise have to go.

- Non-essential costs and employee benefits can be eliminated or postponed.

If a reduction of staff is unavoidable, the company can lay off those employees that will most likely be able to find another job. It may also promise laid-off employees a place in the front row whenever the company starts to hire new staff again.

There are two fundamentally different ways to protect the bottom line: one that makes the CEO a hero in the eyes of the capital markets and another that protects and builds long-term value.

Table 4-2 How to Protect the Bottom Line

Protecting the bottom line for short-term financial performance	Protecting the bottom line for protecting and creating long-term value
Downsizing (job cuts), closing of factories, outsourcing to low-cost countries, divestment of businesses that underperform.	Accepting a temporary drop in profits. Voluntary reduction of salaries, reduction of working hours or increase of hours with no extra pay, insource to keep staff. Eliminate all unnecessary costs.

Most people would argue that the two probably cannot be combined. How can a company educate the financial markets to appreciate long-term value creation? There are three key points:

1. *Be honest.* Tell good news as well as bad news and make no secret the company has problems. Don't make promises you aren't sure you can deliver.

2. *Explain why you chose the difficult road.* For instance, you may roughly quantify the value of the intellectual capital (know-how, know-what, know-why, and know-who) that you want to protect for the future, or you may refer to the company values that you think are more important to hold high than short-term profits.

3. *Make sure you have staff behind you.* Discuss openly with employees and union representatives, and make everyone understand why the plan is for the long-term benefit of the corporation. If you have built up confidence over a number of years, employees will support you all the way and will be even more motivated to work with you.

Analysts and investors are not stupid.

FIRST MEANING—THEN PARTNERSHIP

Partnership is linked to meaning. It makes much more sense to turn the company into one big team if the task is meaningful—for example, "to provide safe, affordable, comfortable, and fast transportation of people" instead of "providing shareholders with a maximum return on their investment." If every employee understands and accepts the meaning of the business and considers himself as an associate rather than an employee, half of the need for day-to-day management and control has gone away.

When the organization has formulated and adopted a meaning beyond just making money and when you have moved employees over to your side of the table, a completely different organizational and management structure becomes possible: the collaborative organization. To know more, look to Chapter 5, "From Hierarchy to Collaboration," for a description of this new organization and Chapter 7 for the hands-on tools to make it a reality.

INDEPENDENT OR INTERDEPENDENT

The partnership between the company and its employees should be extended to suppliers and other external parties as well.

Think of the last time you were preparing the budget. You didn't dare assume that the top line would grow more than 4 percent. With fierce competition, prices probably couldn't be increased at all. Even a 1 percent increase would be noticed by customers, and competition wouldn't hesitate to take advantage. Wages and material costs would most likely go up by 3 percent. Your 56 percent margin would go down. So, why not ask the purchasing department again to face suppliers with an ultimatum: either they reduce price by at least 1 percent or you switch to another supplier.

The large and powerful have practiced this tactic in many cases, and they have actually succeeded in protecting their margin for several years by following that strategy. But in the long term, they probably won't succeed. Most likely, either their suppliers get tired of this show of force or they go bankrupt. There is a limit to how much juice you can squeeze out of one orange.

BE THE BEST IN THE WORLD

One consequence of globalization is that competition becomes less local and more global. You still need to be better than your local competitor, but new competitors from other parts of the world are on their way into your market. Therefore, you need to be the best in the world to do what you do. You can meet that challenge in two ways: Either improve yourself or drop the activity in question and work together with partners that are the best in the world.

No company is large enough to be the best in the world to do everything. Even the largest multinational companies outsource activities such as product development, advertising, manufacturing, logistics, and service functions, including human resource management.

Therefore, an increasing part of the value creation moves from within the company to suppliers and other forms of partners.

Before, companies did virtually everything in-house. Now, the challenge is to find the best possible partners and to establish and develop relationships with partners that generate maximum value. Such partnerships have to be long term, they need to build on exchange of confidential information, and they often require a close cooperation between partner staff and company staff.

In one industry, you may see one company outsourcing anything from component manufacturing, assembly, packaging, supply chain management, distribution, and even product development and sales. Another competitor may keep most of these functions in-house, and both may be successful. The company that keeps most functions in-house can be successful despite its cost disadvantage (for example, of keeping production in high-cost areas if it takes advantage of its highly integrated supply chain). One such electronics company claims that the highly integrated supply chain helps it introduce new products six months quicker than competition. Its industry is highly competitive with product lifetimes of about 12 months, so a six-month advantage is worth more than competition saves on cheap labor in low-cost countries. The point is that this company has become the world champion in innovation and speed in its core business. Secondary functions where speed does not matter to the same extent have been outsourced. For those functions, the company must aim at world leadership in finding subsuppliers and working with them in a mutually beneficial partnership.

The need for partnership extends beyond the supply chain—in particular, toward intermediaries (for example, wholesalers or distributors) and consumers. LEGO, world leader in construction toys, has a community of about two million consumers that build new models and perform competitions. There are not only communities for children, but also for adults (look at www.brickfest.com) to help them share their passion for LEGO. The communities are supported by LEGO, but they operate on an independent basis. Partnership in practice.

Former independent companies, institutions, and consumer groups become interdependent. That's a major change in the mental model.

A NEW MENTAL MODEL

Table 4-3 shows the main differences between the traditional independent company and the interdependence of the networked company.

Table 4-3 Independent Versus Interdependent

	Independent	Interdependent
Perception of business relationship	Fundamentally, a buy-sell relationship in which the two parties are opposites. A win-lose game.	A partnership, which aims at adding maximum value to both businesses. A win-win game.
Information	Limited to the necessary minimum.	As open as possible.
Criterion for success	Minimum purchase price, maximum sales price.	Long-term value creation for all parties involved.
Relation to local community	Minimum interaction.	Extensive interaction and co-operation on social and environmental issues.
Relation to competitors	Enemies that should be fought with all available means.	Competitors, but also potential partners for creating additional value to customers.

The key point is the mental model of how the company and the supplier or partner looks upon each other: Is the relationship a conventional buy-sell relationship or is it a long-term strategic partnership?

In 1776, the first U.S. Congress adopted the Declaration of Independence that marked the liberation of the U.S. from British rule. Independent thinking has ruled the business community for almost 200 years, but in a globalized society, you need to think differently. Perhaps we should write a Declaration of Interdependence, not only for business, but also for society. If we want to continue our creation of wealth, we must increasingly learn to work together, not only by buying and selling to each other, but in a win-win partnership.

BUY-SELL OR WIN-WIN?

Buy-sell relationships are what statisticians call zero-sum games: If I negotiate a better deal for me, you automatically get a worse deal. The sum of your gain or loss and my corresponding gain or loss is constant.

Such arms-length relationships, however, prevent both parties from adapting their offerings and requests to the actual situation of the partner. A house may be built less expensively if the builder understands the business system and cost structure of the suppliers. Dimensions of the building may be adapted to fit the dimensions of available materials, thus reducing waste and processing times. Components for manufacturing may be delivered more cost-efficiently if the supplier has access to the manufacturer's production planning system. Two competitors may both gain advantages if they exchange technologies or allow each other to make use of the other company's patents.

Such relationships should not be zero-sum games. They should be win-win games in which both parties gain advantages and share them.

CORPORATE SOCIAL RESPONSIBILITY

Networking does not need to be restricted only to suppliers, customers, or competitors. The community should also benefit.

Take unemployment. Companies create jobs, but they are not responsible for full employment in the local community. That is the municipality's concern. So far, so good. The point is that companies are also citizens. They are part of the community, so they have an obligation to contribute to reducing unemployment. This is true, in general, but particularly important in relation to disadvantaged people. Therefore, companies must establish partnerships with the community to help create jobs for the physically, socially, or mentally disadvantaged. This may be done by establishing protected workshops where the disadvantaged can perform processes that are less demanding.

Grundfos, the world-leading manufacturer of pumping systems, maintains that at least 3 percent of its employees must be disadvantaged to the extent that they would not otherwise be able to get a job. The cost is considerable, but minimal in a larger context. The benefit, however, is big: The local community wants to do everything it can to support Grundfos and employees change their perception of Grundfos—not an opposite, but a partner. Grundfos does not engage in corporate social responsibility to gain advantages from community, but because it is an essential part of the culture of its family-owned company. Grundfos recognizes that by being socially responsible, it gains many advantages from local communities, employees, and unions, and from customers that like to do business with a socially responsible company.

Take a moment to reflect on your perception of business. Most likely, you came out of a tradition where the purpose of business is to make money for shareholders. Full stop. But are you sure that this mental model is ideal today? Does it take into account the notion of corporate citizenship? Are corporations citizens? Can a business that focuses only on one goal, profit to the shareholders, attract and retain the best employees in the industry long term?

PARTNER WITH COMPETITION?

The idea of partnership with suppliers, customers, and local community is not new. It is a well-established tradition in many countries. But partnering with competition is rare. Why partner with your enemy?

There are good reasons to partner with competition, and if you play openly and pass on a fair share of the advantage to customers, the antitrust authorities in most countries will allow you to do so. Think of patents, for example. If you have a valuable patent, why not exchange rights to use it with a similarly valuable patent from your competitor? Unless the two of you cover the entire world market combined, you both gain a major advantage against the rest of competition at no cost. You may even expand the market for your technology because a novel approach is accepted quicker by consumers if more than one company markets it. It becomes a new category instead of just a new product.

Competitors may also gain significant advantages by defining standards together: In the hearing aid industry, four competitors jointly defined the future hardware and software standards for programming the next generation digital hearing aids. The rest of the industry had no choice but joining the standard, leaving the four competitors in the driver's seat for several years and saving clinics millions of dollars that would otherwise have been invested in multiple programming systems from different manufacturers. Everyone wins except those competitors that were not innovative enough to get this idea and implement it.

Teaming up with competition is a taboo to many managers, partly because legislation to prevent any limitations to free competition is in place in most countries. But competitors may team up in many ways that do not hamper competition, and good cooperation among competitors may help avoid unnecessary costs of doing business and lead to lower prices, higher consumption, and more profit. Competitors may exchange intellectual property rights such as patents, and competitors may also cooperate in creating a joint infrastructure, which may save money for all involved without limiting competition.

 Are you willing to think the unthinkable and consider cooperation with competitors?

Networking with suppliers, customers, and academia becomes much easier if the company has a clear meaning. It is the meaning that unites the network. It serves as inspiration for all participants, and it helps to align interests.

MEANING COUNTS

Networking—that is, partnership with external bodies—also links to partnership thinking within the company. In a networked business, many employees are in contact with external partners. Employees constantly exchange information and make decisions that cannot be micromanaged from company management. If employees consider themselves partners, there is no need for such micromanagement.

FOOD FOR THOUGHT

Think of the relationship between management and staff in your organization:

- How would you describe it?
- How do you think your employees would describe it?
- Give three examples of genuine partnership thinking from the company's point of view.
- Give three examples where employees act like associates rather than partners.
- What is the greatest obstacle for turning the relationship between the company and employees into a genuine partnership? The employees? The labor unions? The management? The board of directors? The owners?
- Think of one initiative you can take to move the relationship one step further toward partnership.

Think of how your organization deals with external partners such as suppliers, knowledge centers, intermediaries, and consumers:

- How would you describe each relationship?
- Are you partners or opposites? In other words, which relationships are zero-sum and which are win-win?
- What would be the most attractive possible alliance with competition? Who would object it? What would the likely benefit be for your organization, for the competitors, and for consumers?

5

From Hierarchy to Collaboration

TAKE A LOOK AT A "NORMAL" ORGANIZATION

Think about a department in your organization or some other organization you know—10 to 50 employees. What probably comes to your mind is an office or laboratory environment, perhaps one floor of a building, and probably a boss with a separate office—most likely a male boss with a mixture of men and women on the staff.

The whole thing is most likely pretty well organized. Everyone has his or her functions, and life in the office today probably doesn't differ much from yesterday. Everyone looks pretty busy with his or her files, binders, and computer screens. There are pictures of children and pets on the desk. Yellow paper notes here and there to remember names, tasks, and procedures. Work may be somewhat boring, but there are good colleagues to talk to, there is free coffee, the lunch break is nice, and eight hours pass quickly, and you are ready to go home or to go out.

That's how most departments are. They do the job they are supposed to do reasonably well, the boss is busy, and the company is doing okay, so far.

Most likely, such organizations are well on their way into the downward part of the first cycle. The dynamism that prevailed when the organization was young and made its way up the first cycle has disappeared. The organization most likely has forgotten that it was that dynamism that initially pushed it up the first cycle.

If you are a manager, you have a choice: Either do the job more or less the way everyone else does or make a difference. Either ride on the downward part of the first cycle with the rest of the business or create a new second cycle. You may look differently upon your life, but isn't your life too short not to try to make a difference? Isn't your life too short to consider work only as a means to make a living? If you are in charge of a department, why not find out how to make it the best department in the world? Why not start the second cycle there? You can do it for the challenge, you can do it for the organization and for the staff, or you can do it to have fun yourself! Here is what I would do: go collaboration!

 Take a moment to reflect on your own achievements as a manager. If someone were to write a 1,000-page book on management in the last 100 years in your country, have you done anything worth mentioning? Did you attend the same business school, do you go to the same conferences, and do you read the same books as your peers? If yes, no wonder you create nothing really different from them.

DESIGN FOR STABILITY OR CHANGE?

Most conventional organizations are designed for stability. Their business is to get something done with maximum impact, with a minimum of errors, and at the lowest possible cost. Ever since the assembly line was invented in the automobile industry, the answer to this challenge has been specialization. Every single employee becomes an expert in what she does and is backed by computer systems, rules, and procedures. The inventor was Frederick Winslow Taylor, an American production engineer. His idea of specialization was great for large manufacturing operations, but management theory has recognized for decades that this *Tayloristic* approach does not work well for knowledge-intensive organizations that need a greater perspective and more flexibility and creativity in their work. However, despite the fact that this organizational approach is long overdue, it survives remarkably well. There are even union people who argue that stability and specialization is the best possible way to work. It gives the individual job security, and it frees him from wearing out during work. It reduces the risk that the employee takes problems from work home with him.

The logical workplace design to match this type of office work is the individual office or cubicle design. The office was designed to provide a quiet and pleasant place to work for the individual. It was financial restrictions that prevented every employee to have an office, which would take up too much space and would be too expensive. Therefore, individual offices originally became a privilege for the bosses only. Later, more senior employees and specialists got offices, but in most cases, the cubicle was chosen as a low-cost alternative.

Your future workplace should be nothing like an office or a large space with cubicles. In all likelihood, your job and your colleagues' jobs will be nothing like the specialized routine function they were yesterday. Your day will most likely be very different from yesterday, and you will tend to forget the clock at the time you would normally be leaving work. If you manage to get to this point, your department or company will do a very different and a much better job than today.

It starts with your ambition to do an outstanding job as a leader. If in the past you did 100 transactions a day, if you had 6 percent dissatisfied customers, or if your turnaround time was two weeks, don't go for a 10 percent improvement. Go for a 100 percent improvement or more—that is, 200 transactions a day, less than 1 percent dissatisfied customers, or a two-day turnaround time. That's what it takes to stimulate the innovative capability of yourself and your team.

Next, realize that dramatic change always requires simultaneous change of several factors. You can change seven aspects of your organization simultaneously:

1. Change your own role: Behave as a leader rather than a manager.

2. Make everyone do several different jobs simultaneously (multijob).

3. Take away the conventional hierarchical structure and substitute it with a smart structure (collaboration, described in the remainder of this chapter).

4. Make work a team effort rather than an individual effort.

5. Make change and continuous learning the name of the game.

6. Create a mechanism to reward exactly the behavior you desire.

7. Design the office for maximum relevant interaction, stimulus, and fun.

TEST YOUR OWN ATTITUDES

 Before going deeper into each of these points, try to answer these 10 questions with a yes or no. Questions are phrased as though you are a manager:

1. In your job as a manager, is it important that you always know where your employees are and what they are doing?

2. Do you try to motivate your employees to focus on one task at a time?

3. If you want to correct the way one of your employees works, do you normally ask her supervisor to do it?

4. If there is a problem with the behavior of some employees, do you write a memo to all employees that clarify the company rules?

5. If you have some important information to pass on to the employees, do you call your management team together and inform them so that they can inform the employees of their respective departments?

6. In a constantly changing world, do you think that the organization should respond to change by reorganizing—for example, once every year or once every two years?

7. Are you normally concerned to make a task a team effort because it might take away accountability?

8. Do you think it is basically a good idea that employee salaries vary with education, organizational level, and seniority?

9. Do you think that an organization should preferably have a certain structure in order to make sure the job gets done and to give employees the security in their daily work?

10. Would you rather avoid organizational changes if they were not really necessary to make sure organization does the job?

Count your yes answers to the 10 questions. If you had three or more yes answers, you probably need to reconsider your mental model for an organization. You may be influenced too deeply by classical "manufacturing" thinking. Perhaps you should consider some collaboration thinking for your organization.

WHY COLLABORATION?

When I first worked on designing a truly collaborative organization, somebody suggested that we used the term *spaghetti* to illustrate it. Spaghetti is a metaphor to picture a new type of organization that is probably quite foreign to you. In the dry form, spaghetti is stiff and really not worth eating. The taste is sort of neutral, and there is little excitement with it. Dried spaghetti is dead stuff. But after a few minutes of boiling, spaghetti may become part of many different and very tasty pasta dishes. There is no clear (hierarchical) structure in the dish and each part of the spaghetti connects to the rest in its own way. It moves constantly. It is alive.

If the task of an organization were to produce exactly the same items in exactly same little boxes day after day, the ideal organization would probably look like a machine. It would have clear structures and a well-defined hierarchy. But mass production is not the task of most organizations today. Most organizations today are in business to not only provide output, but also to respond to different customer needs and constantly adapt themselves to changing needs and environments. That's why they should look more like spaghetti. To take it further, they should look more like the human brain. After all, does the human brain not look a little like well-boiled spaghetti?

Table 5-1 From Hierarchy to Collaboration

	Hierarchy	Collaboration
Your role	Manager	Leader
Job	Management defines each specific job with clear tasks, authority, superiors, collaborators, and subordinates. Management identifies and appoints the person that fits the job as closely as possible. Training serves as a means to compensate for minor misfits between employee and job description.	Each staff member creates his own portfolio of tasks according to company priorities and personal interests and qualifications. Staff members are urged to choose some tasks outside their formal qualifications. Jobs change constantly.
Structure	The formal organization constitutes one hierarchy, which is supported by staff functions at various organizational levels.	The company is run by an informal organization, which comprises three mutually interacting structures: project, people, and profession.
Nature of work	An individual effort with the primary purpose of making money for yourself.	A team effort to serve a combination of personal, company, and societal interests.
Change	The organization is stable over periods of time. When there is a perceived need for change, management designs the new organization secretly and implements the change.	The organization changes constantly, and change is considered a normal part of daily life in the organization. Staff initiates most changes, and many changes take place without management involvement.
Rewards	Employees are rewarded according to a negotiated pay scale and incentive system. There are clear rules for working hours, overtime, and benefits.	Staff rewards are fully individual. They are determined according to an interactive process, which includes peer review. Rules for working hours and so on are reduced to a minimum.
Workplace	The workplace primarily provides physical protection from noise and other disturbing factors.	The workplace is an essential part of organizational culture. It provides the best possible physical framework for individual and teamwork, and it stimulates innovation.

CHANGE YOUR OWN ROLE: BEHAVE AS A LEADER RATHER THAN A MANAGER

Fifty or 100 years ago, a manager was a person who organized the work of others, who told others what to do, how to do it, and when they were supposed to be finished. The manager also controlled the work of the employees along the road and finally accepted the result. That was a relevant way to do it, in particular because most workers were badly educated and most jobs were relatively well defined and straightforward.

Today, most of those straightforward and well-defined jobs are gone. They have been moved to low-cost countries, or they will soon be taken over by robots and computer systems. The jobs that are left require employees to think, to be creative, and to be flexible. That's why they need to be performed in a different type of environment by a different form of people who are led in a different fashion. *Knowledge workers* need more leadership and less management.

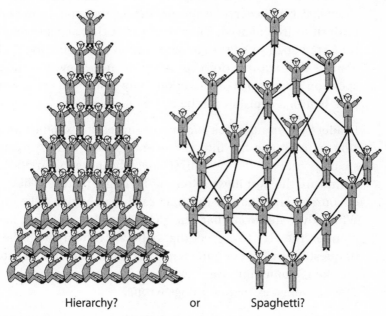

Hierarchy?   or   Spaghetti?

Figure 5-1

Contrary to managers, leaders do not just tell the employee what to do and how to do it, but they tell the employee what needs to be done, why, and when. They leave the employee freedom to choose how to do the job—obviously, within the limitations of the capabilities of the employee and current business processes of the firm. They also facilitate involvement of colleagues in the job and encourage the employee to learn from others and share his experiences with others. They stay available for counseling during the job, they keep an eye on the process, but they only interfere if something important seems to go wrong.

Leaders set the direction. They listen to all relevant stakeholders, and they strive to balance their different and more or less well-justified needs in a fair manner. They focus on the things that really matter, and they do not hide the fact that they make choices and set priorities. They willingly discuss their reasons for choosing, and they are open for modifications of the course if arguments are sufficiently convincing. They are firm, yet open.

Leaders go out of their way to create a consensus among staff. They insist that everyone accepts the current course and priorities until they are changed. They tend to get that acceptance because they stay open to new arguments and new information that might change the picture. However, they do not allow too much time spent on discussions on direction; they insist that some time must pass before a decision can be challenged again.

Leaders constantly look for opportunities to explain how a decision or a choice fits into the overall strategy. They relate even small points to the overall strategy because often those small points are the best illustrations of the larger picture. They publicly encourage all behavior that moves things in the right direction. When they discover that one person behaves in an inadequate manner, they try to correct that behavior directly with the person in question instead of punishing everyone. They try to catch people doing something right, whereas managers primarily look for those employees that do things wrong.

Leaders accept mistakes. They even encourage the employees that make mistakes to discuss them and to ask for help from their colleagues to do the right thing next time. They focus on learning instead of punishment. They consider an employee that has made a major mistake to be a major asset, and they look upon the cost of the mistake as an investment in the person who made it.

Take a moment to characterize yourself. Are you a leader or a manager? Try the questions that follow, and check out Table 5-2:

- What is most important to you?
  a) To meet your key performance indicators (bonus criteria).
  b) To build a great business.
- How do you decide upon salary adjustments for your employees?
  a) I make sure we match available statistics based on education and seniority.
  b) I pay employees based on the value of their work for the organization.
- Your boss asks you to reduce staff by one person in next year's budget.
  a) I find the person that I think we could best do without.
  b) I take a hard look at our business to find out if reducing staff is the right decision. If I think another option would be better, I will try to change my boss' decision.
- One of your employees suggests an attractive new business idea that is not in this year's budget. Do you:
  a) Wait until next year's budget will allow for it.
  b) Help develop the idea so you both can present it for your boss in order to get money to implement it now.
- Two of your employees work on a task that would be better served by belonging to another department. Would you:
  a) Keep the task in your hands not to reduce your position and power.
  b) Propose that the project was transferred to where it belongs.

If you answer a) to two or more of these questions, you are probably more of a manager than a leader—that is, you have something to work on. After you have learned to behave like a leader rather than a manager, you are ready for the change.

Table 5-2 Manager or Leader?

	Manager	Leader
Primary function	Keep the company well organized and efficient.	Keep the company disorganized and innovative—and still efficient.
Job	Analyze, plan, organize, inform, direct, follow up, and reward.	Share information, set direction, establish consensus, stimulate action, orchestrate processes, reward, and balance long-term and short-term goals.
Relation to subordinates	Make decisions, control progress, and evaluate performance; reward, hire, and fire.	Share information, collaborate, stimulate, inspire, and serve staff members with the aim of creating maximum value for the organization and personal growth for the individual.
Relation to superiors	Serve the needs of the boss, execute orders, and provide information.	Share information, collaborate, and challenge conventional wisdom.
Qualifications	Professional skills and relevant experience, authority, initiative, and decision-making skills.	Process skills, empathy, vision, communication and coaching skills, and integrity.

MAKE EVERYONE DO SEVERAL DIFFERENT JOBS SIMULTANEOUSLY (MULTIJOB)

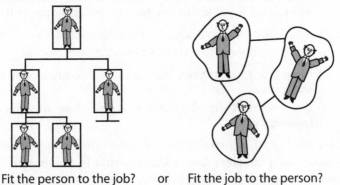

Fit the person to the job?   or   Fit the job to the person?

Figure 5-2

The idea is simply that you motivate—or even force, if necessary—every employee to do at least two things that he is not formally qualified to do as part of his job. In other words, every employee should continue his current job, but in addition to that job, everyone should find two or more new things to do. It sounds a bit silly, but you will be surprised of the effect: When employees are encouraged to do something new, most argue that they can only do what they are formally qualified to do. For example, the engineer stays with construction and the bookkeeper sticks to the numbers. But then, ask the engineers what they do in their spare time. One may be a tennis trainer, another may be a do-it-yourself person, or one may travel to visit a friend in France. So what could they do for the firm? Train customers of fellow employees. Write user instructions or manuals for the firm's products or assist with sales in France. Virtually every employee has resources that the firm does not know about and does not currently tap into.

You may accept this point, but why on earth should you invite or force an engineer to help sell products in France when the company actually is short of engineering resources? There are very good reasons for that. Engineers who spend all their time in engineering develop a narrow view of the world and of the firm. They tend to think that all problems can be solved if everyone would think just like themselves. They look upon salespeople and customers as second-class citizens that don't appreciate the highly qualified work of the engineers.

If they go to France to work with the salespeople there, they start to look upon the world in general, and the firm in particular, from a different angle. They discover that engineering solutions don't always work with customers the way they were supposed to. They realize that customers may prefer the much simpler and less advanced solution from a competitor because they really don't need all the features that the engineers have built into your company's product. They realize that perception often wins over reality. They gain respect for the work of the salesperson, which makes them listen more carefully next time a salesperson provides feedback from the market. Their mono view of the world has become a stereo one. They have become better engineers by stepping out of their engineering role for a period of time.

But how do tight time schedules in the engineering department allow the engineer to spend two or four weeks in France? That isn't a problem. Who wouldn't like to go to France for two or four weeks, in particular, if one's significant other lived there? Make it a reward if a certain project is finished on time. And throw in an extra week of vacation or a couple of weekend trips to the Riviera. The next time an opportunity arises to go somewhere to work with the sales staff, there will be five engineers applying!

In some cases, you have to use some sort of force to push professionals "out of the box." The most efficient way is to first motivate positively and, if that isn't enough, to offer a cleaning or dishwashing job in the company cafeteria as a possible second or third job. Most professionals then accept that they can do something else. Frankly speaking, it doesn't really matter what that "something else" is. It is the opportunity to experience the organization from two or three different angles that makes the difference, not the angles themselves. It is also the opportunity to add a fresh perspective to what the company does in other areas. Few innovations come from people that have been doing the same thing for many years. Nothing can substitute a fresh look from someone with a different background.

After such a multijob scheme has been established, make sure it is maintained. Invite employees to share their experiences with other staff at company or department meetings. Make them tell what they learned and how their perceptions of the company were changed. Force them to propose how the work of their "new" department could be improved if their experience was applied to the new department. Make them think of how their own work could be improved bearing in mind what they just experienced.

Multijob organizations gain fourfold:

- Employees take up new challenges while continuing their current jobs. This liberates new resources to tackle problems.
- Employees inspire their new colleagues by bringing a different approach and asking new questions. At the same time, they get inspired to do their main job in a different fashion.
- Cross-functional links are greatly strengthened. Employees gain respect for each other and develop links that prevent misunderstandings and double efforts.

- Employees become more content and have more fun in their jobs. They develop within their jobs and within the company, they have opportunities to try new challenges, and they tend to stay longer in the firm. And you as a leader get a unique opportunity to figure out who has potential and who has not.

Think of yourself and the resources you could bring to your organization. Your formal education and your work experience define what you are formally qualified to do. I suggest you write down three and five qualifications that you have outside of what you are formally qualified to do. Think of your spare-time activities. Were you once a Scout leader? Were you ever a coach, or did you ever do any volunteer work? Are you organizing parties or other events within your church or neighborhood? Are you interested in art or architecture? Are you a good cook? Most people have a wealth of capabilities that are never used at their workplace. Hierarchies, job descriptions, departmental silos, and conventional thinking are the factors that prevent employees and managers to enrich their jobs and their companies.

Take away the conventional hierarchical structure and substitute it with a smart structure.

Hierarchies are instruments to direct and to control. But with the exception of war and similar situations, conventional command structures are poor instruments to lead a high-performance organization.

The need is for managers to think the unthinkable and simply discard the formal hierarchical structure of the organization. No departments, no job titles on business cards, no organizational chart whatsoever. You will be surprised how well you can do without these former necessities and how much you have saved.

Saving money is not the prime objective, but take a moment and calculate roughly how much the hierarchical management structure of your department or your company actually costs:

- Count the high salaries, bonus schemes, stock option programs, and social costs of managers.
- Add the cost of assistants, secretaries, company cars, computers, phones, and travel budgets.

- Make an estimate of the time that managers take from other people, preparing reports and statistics, making plans and budgets, discussing deviations and corrective actions, and participating in endless meetings.

The total cost of the management structure may add up to 20 percent or more of the capacity costs of a firm.

Table 5-3 can help you make a rough estimate of the cost of the hierarchical management structure of your organization. Take one department as an example.

Table 5-3 Worksheet for Determining Cost of Hierarchical Management

Cost item	Annual cost
Salaries, including social costs, bonuses, and other benefits	
Salaries of executive assistants and all other support staff, including all costs	
Costs of computers, communication equipment, company cars, and the budget for travel and executive education	
The time spent on employees preparing reports and statistics, making plans and budgets, analyzing and discussing deviations, and corrective actions times the average cost per employee	
Total gross expense related to the management function	
Total employee related cost for the department	
Gross expense in percent of the total employee related cost for the department	

You might well reach a percentage of management costs that adds up to 25 percent or more of total employee related costs for the department. How does that compare with the value that management adds to the work of the department?

Imagine that you could do without that cost. You might be able to add 10 percentage points to the return on sales. You would be the industry leader. You could self-finance all investments. You could invest in developing the staff.

You can.

The key is to discover and utilize the informal organization that exists in every single firm. In every firm, the management task has three aspects that do not need to be taken care of by the same people. Actually, the organization benefits from having these tasks assigned to different people who are not full-time managers.

The three aspects are as follows:

- *Projects*. Call every task of the organization a project—even those that repeat on an ongoing basis. Identify one person (the project leader) that may naturally be put in charge of each project. Many persons end up being in charge of several projects, but there also are junior employees or specialists who are not in charge. Identify a number of project owners (for example, perhaps five people in an organization of 300 people and 100 projects). Project owners keep themselves informed about a number of projects and interfere if something important seems to go wrong. If all project owners are together, the entire knowledge of what goes on in the firm is present. This way, every employee is part of one or more projects. Later, allow employees to join new projects of their own choice, after they have completed current assignments.

- *Professions*. Identify all the professions that the company needs to master in order to carry out its work. In a commercial company, professions would probably include sales and marketing, product and business development, supply chain management (including purchasing, manufacturing, and logistics), quality management, knowledge management, finance, administration, and service. For each profession, identify one guru (or professional coordinator) who knows the profession best. The role of the guru is to continuously develop the profession, inspire staff within the profession to maintain and develop high standards and methods, and control that everything done within the profession meets company professional standards. Make every employee choose which professions he wants to be associated with.

- *People*. Make every employee choose one senior person to serve as a mentor or people manager for the employee. Do the necessary shuffling and pooling so you have about one mentor per 10 to 15 people. Make it the job of the mentor to serve as a coach that helps and inspires the employee to do her best. If legal or other requirements force the company to have a formal "manager" for every employee, let the mentor serve that role. This means that employees themselves choose their bosses. Make the mentor responsible for performance and pay review and allow employees to choose a new mentor if they so desire.

None of the functions in the preceding list are full time. They are second or third jobs.

There is a tremendous gain in substituting the formal hierarchy with distributed leadership as outlined here. The company saves significant costs, the best specialists that were once promoted to management positions can now return to specialist or other roles that are directly linked to the mainstream business. Employees are empowered to focus on creating results instead of serving their managers.

The order of magnitude of the potential gain of this collaboration structure varies greatly from one organization to the other, but it might be very large. However, it only works if it is combined with the other three bases for the second cycle: meaning, partnership, and value-based leadership. Doubling overall value creation is not out of the question. In my first attempt, I went for a 30 percent productivity improvement within three years. The actual result was cutting the administrative overhead into about half and growing sales with more than 50 percent.

Take a little while to reflect what this could mean for your organization. What could you achieve if the current workload could be covered by 20 percent less employees? What could you do if 20 percent of your employees was freed to constantly improve the quality of what the organization does and to continue improving its productivity?

The sky is the limit.

MAKE WORK A TEAM EFFORT RATHER THAN AN INDIVIDUAL EFFORT

Conventional organizations tend to view the relationship between the employee and the employer primarily as a one-to-one deal according to a combination of individual and collective agreements. For example, the employee is a member of a department, but if he becomes ill, it is the task of management to find a substitute for him while he is absent.

This does not necessarily need to be so. Simply make it the responsibility of the employee to make sure that the job gets done, even if the employee is absent because of illness, vacation, education, second or third jobs, or something else. Ask the employee to arrange for another person to fill the job when needed. Some jobs require more than one substitute, but leave that decision to the individual employee. It is her responsibility to make sure that the job is done every single day.

You will be surprised that this is perfectly possible. The employees can agree to substitute for each other. If one becomes ill, he does not just call the company, but he calls his colleague to stand in. This actually reduces absence and indeed reduces the need for temporary labor. Those who substitute experience second and third jobs, perhaps bringing in their own substitutes, if necessary.

Trusting all employees to find their own substitutes also makes the company much less vulnerable if key employees choose to leave. There is always a substitute that knows the job. You may question whether employees are actually paid for performing what normally is perceived as a management task. It is true that planning for substitutes used to be a management task, but the point is that this is not necessary. Employees get better and better informed. They demand higher salaries and wages. Why should they not plan for their own absence?

If you follow the preceding advice to name every task a project with one responsible leader, you may add another feature to promote teamwork: Make employees themselves choose which project groups they want to be part of.

That leads to two consequences:

- Some projects will be overstaffed because they are perceived to be more attractive than others, or perhaps the project leader is a particularly attractive person to work with. Always give the project leader the right to say no thanks. But if the project becomes overstaffed anyway, you may simply choose to live with that because it will lead to faster completion and higher quality due to the high motivation of the team involved.

- Other projects will be understaffed, either because the project appears to be less interesting or because the leader is not a good one. That's good for the company: Less attractive projects are usually less important and perhaps you should consider outsourcing the task or you should consider eliminating it completely. Less attractive project leaders should be motivated to become specialists where they will probably make a much greater contribution to the business.

Leave it to your staff to choose what to do in order to make the maximum contribution to the business. If you have an adequate mechanism to reward the behavior you really want, you will be in good shape.

These points illustrate that knowledge work is quite different from conventional industrial work. Table 5-4 summarizes this point.

Table 5-4 Work Is Not What It Used to Be

	Industrial work	Knowledge work
Content	One task at a time.	Multiple tasks simultaneously.
Time	Work takes place within well-defined working hours. Overtime is paid according to collective agreement.	Any time. Staff member is not paid for time, but rather for the contribution he makes to the company.
Allocation of people to jobs	Management decides on allocation based upon employee skills and company priorities.	Staff members decide according to company priorities and personal preferences. Staff members establish contract with project leader and seek acceptance from guru (professional coordinator).
Priority of tasks	Management decides.	Staff members decide after discussion with project leader and others.
Organizational context	Employee is an individual that works for the company through employment in a department.	The staff member is part of constantly changing teams that perform a variety of tasks that lead toward a common goal. The company as such, not a specific department, is the employer.
Appointment of leaders	Upper management decides.	Staff members decide which leaders they want to work for. If a project leader cannot gather a team, she must find something else to do.
Workplace	Stable over time.	Constantly changing according to current tasks.
Communication	Information is given on a need-to-know basis.	Information and knowledge flows freely.

MAKE CHANGE AND CONTINUOUS LEARNING THE NAME OF THE GAME

If you have substituted the conventional departments with projects and if you have converted managers into drivers for the mainstream business, you have at the same time removed most of the barriers to change. In general, managers are in favor of change if it strengthens their own position. Almost all changes also have losers that will counteract the change, which is another reason to take away the conventional management structure.

When a new challenge arises, just define a project, look for a project leader, and let her find the people to join the team, perhaps initially as their second and third jobs, but later as their first jobs after they have completed their current primary job or found a substitute for it. If something fundamental changes, just redefine the relevant projects and let the staff reconfigure. If you are able to explain the logic behind the change and the importance of it, you can rest assured that your staff will understand the message and focus accordingly. Once, I had to completely reshuffle a group of almost 200 staff to meet a changed market situation for my company. We realized the need for change on Friday, thought it over during the weekend, announced the plan at a meeting for all staff on Monday, pooled together the staff response on Wednesday, and did a complete change on Friday, including a physical movement of almost every employee. To celebrate the new organization, we organized a big party Friday night and off we were for the new challenge on Monday morning. Such ability to change is one of the strongest competitive weapons a company can have.

The resistance to change goes away if change is made part of every day's work. If you do a quick change, you often make a few mistakes. When you have identified them, correct them quickly, and your staff will be even more confident to take part in the next change.

Constantly changing team structures, gurus in charge of professional development, sharing jobs outside traditional departmental barriers, and a completely open environment creates the ideal environment for continuous learning, improvement, and innovation. Learning and innovation take place when different professions (e.g., engineers and anthropologists) interact rather than within a specific profession itself. If you want a really new product, you will most likely be disappointed if you ask the same team of engineers to do the job that did the current model. The team may make it a little smaller, smarter, or cheaper, but it will seldom break the rules and come forward with a real innovation. Real progress comes from the interplay between people with different backgrounds: customers, salespeople, engineers, marketing people, psychologists, anthropologists, men and women, Christians, Hindus, Muslims, experienced people, and novices.

It is this constantly changing interplay between people with different backgrounds in an open, flexible, and stimulating environment that creates the innovation capability that large, mature, and successful companies lose on their way up the first cycle. The good news is that it can be recreated to serve as a platform for the second cycle.

Table 5-5 summarizes the point.

Table 5-5 Change Becomes the Name of the Game

	Hierarchy	Collaboration
Frequency of change	Stability over periods of time and changes inbetween as required by changing internal or external conditions.	Change is constant and takes place in small steps every day.
Magnitude of change	Predominantly large changes.	Predominantly small changes.
Decision and involvement	Management decides when to change, what to change, and how to change. Employees are involved in execution of change.	Staff decides most changes without the involvement of leaders.
Information	Management maintains secrecy about potential changes while preparation is in progress. Information is given immediately before the change is executed.	Because change is constant, there is complete openness about it.
Level of uncertainty	In stable periods, there is little uncertainty. But as the need for change builds up, there may be great uncertainty, which occupies much mental energy of both employees and management.	Constantly high, but not perceived as an issue.
Learning	Formalized and initiated by management. Focused on few key areas in the company.	Ongoing, informal, and widespread due to constantly changing teams and openness.

CREATE A MECHANISM TO REWARD EXACTLY THE BEHAVIOR YOU DESIRE

Conventional first cycle thinking most often leads companies, labor unions, and professional associations to settle for compensation schemes that are "objective"—that is, based on generally accepted objected and measurable criteria. Managers often argue that such schemes reduce the amount of noise in the bargaining process, which can often be very time consuming.

Consider a completely different approach, which may take most of the fuzz out of salary adjustments: set up a *mechanism* for salary adjustments rather than an agreed pay scale according to objective criteria.

The mechanism has five phases:

1. Ask the employee to explain to his mentor how he has made a contribution to the company within the last 12 months. Invite him to include everything—even such things as his contribution to the company barbecue and helping a colleague out of a difficult situation.

2. Let the mentor perform a reality check by talking informally to colleagues of the employee and people he has cooperated with during the last 12 months—obviously, with a main focus on internal and external "customers" of the employee.

3. The mentor reviews the current salary level of the employee in light of available internal and external statistics to determine if there is a special need to adjust the level to match the market. Based on this review, the mentor draws up a recommended salary adjustment.

4. At a monthly meeting, all mentors meet to discuss salary adjustments for those employees that were originally employed in the month in question. In other words, employees are reviewed in their anniversary month, which means that about one twelfth of the staff is reviewed each month. Mentors decide the adjustment for each employee in question by consensus only.

5. Following the decision, the mentors meet with their respective employees and explain the outcome of the reality check and the reasons that formed the basis for the conclusion of the mentors. If the employee disagrees with the conclusion, he is perfectly free to choose another mentor for next year. No appeal possible for this year.

The advantage of this procedure is that it is objective and fair, yet completely individual. The employees have chosen their mentors and are free to choose another one next year. The mentors have listened to the input from the employees and have combined that with input from peers and statistics. The group of mentors makes the actual decision. Nobody can challenge the fairness and objectivity of the procedure. Salary adjustment quickly moves to become an insignificant part of the company agenda. Negotiations with unions turn into dialogue where overall company salary levels are compared with industry statistics.

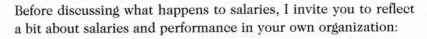

Before discussing what happens to salaries, I invite you to reflect a bit about salaries and performance in your own organization:

- Look upon a certain group of professionals—for example, service engineers, executive secretaries, or department managers.

- Try to estimate their relative contribution to the organization. Use 100 as an index for the lowest performing person in one category and assign an index number to each other person within the same category. If you think the value of the work of another person is three times as high as the bottom one, assign 300 as the index figure.

- Calculate a similar index figure for salaries and compare the two. In most cases, you will find that value of contribution to the organization varies much more than salaries. It is not unusual the people that are five or 10 times as important for the company are paid only 30 to 50 percent higher than the lowest performing employee in the same category.

That's exactly what the proposed mechanism for salary adjustment does (see Table 5-6). It means a big change compared to conventional "objective" scales and agreements: Traditional department heads will most likely lose, in particular, if they have not yet reestablished themselves as top specialists deeply involved in mainstream business. Highly visible, self-promoting, and often superficial employees lose if they don't make a real and genuine contribution to the organization. Top specialists tend to gain because they turn out to be of much greater value than what was perceived previously. The superb project leader gains and former office assistants or secretaries that have now become excellent customer service representatives or project coordinators also gain significantly. The average or below average engineer loses. The spread goes up significantly, which is fair because the value of a superb employee may be five or 10 times that of an average or below average employee.

High salaries for high performers and low salaries for low performers reduce attrition. The best people can't get a higher pay elsewhere. The weakest people can't get a job anywhere else and if they manage to get one, who bothers—particularly if they get employed by a competitor.

Table 5-6 A Reward Mechanism Instead of a Pay Scale

	Hierarchy	Collaboration
Pay scale	Negotiated through collective bargaining.	No pay scale.
Focus of the bargaining process	Balance demands from staff against market conditions and company needs. A win-lose battle.	Provide reviewer with comprehensive and balanced information about total staff member contribution to the company.
Behavior	Maximize positive impression on the superior.	Maximize positive contribution to the company in broad sense.
Spread in distribution of rewards	Low spread in general. Spread mostly generated by management position, seniority, and formal education.	High spread, mostly generated by overall contribution to the company and hard work.
Likely winners in salary game	Upper management, employees with higher education and other formal qualifications, and people who please their boss.	Superb specialists, efficient project leaders, and former office staff that have changed from assistant roles to own functions.
Likely losers in salary game	Hardworking, less visible specialists and assistants.	Former middle managers that have had difficulties finding a productive function in the less formal organization.

DESIGN THE OFFICE FOR MAXIMUM RELEVANT INTERACTION, STIMULUS, AND FUN

Whereas conventional offices were designed to provide quietness and room for concentrated individual work, the workplace of the second cycle looks completely different. It should be designed for maximum relevant interaction, stimulus, and fun (see Table 5-7).

The short version of that story follows. If you take the point that innovation and customization is the essence of competitiveness in the future, you have to accept that the workplace should be designed for maximum relevant interaction among staff. If employees in a particular department are located next to each other in an open office environment, they may often disturb each other because they perform their tasks oriented toward different customers or projects. And the interaction they have is narrow in the sense that interaction between people with similar backgrounds seldom leads to innovation.

However, when working on a project together, interaction between people with highly different backgrounds is different than the interaction between those with similar backgrounds. That interaction is constructive. It leads to a variety of inputs to the work of everyone in the group, and it provides an excellent environment for learning. Intercultural and cross-functional interaction is a major source of strength.

That's why workplaces should have no defined offices. Moreover, no employee should sit at the same place for too long. Everyone should move when she becomes involved in other projects, and those who have several jobs at the same time should be able to move several times every day. This goes in particular for leaders. They should be involved in more or less everything that goes on; therefore, they have the greatest need for being in the center of everything.

To make this vision a reality takes considerable thinking and a lot of work. If the workplace is to become really mobile, computer systems should be good enough to virtually eliminate the need for paper. All filing should be electronic, and mechanisms need to be designed to actually foster constant movement, which does not come by itself.

Table 5-7 Two Different Views on Workplace Design

	Industrial	Collaboration
Primary design criterion	Protect employees from being disturbed by others.	Ensure maximum interaction between staff members, in particular those with different backgrounds that work on joint projects.
Preferred physical layout	Office environment for upper management and high-level specialists. Cubicles for lower-level staff. Environment is homogeneous with matching colors, light, and so on.	Completely open; however, not in large spaces. Different barriers, including plants and trees, break open space. Great variation in colors, decoration, art, light, and sound environment. Many smaller breakout rooms for temporary individual or team use.
Typical time spent at location	Years.	Hours or days.
Management	Located in separate offices in separate section (the executive floor).	Located in between ordinary staff, frequently changing.
Barrier to change	High.	Low.

IT CAN BE DONE

It takes guts to establish such a collaboration organization, even if you have achieved the backing of your boss. Be prepared for staff to pay lip service to it. Be prepared for labor unions to object to it. Be prepared for middle managers to work against it and for your colleagues in other companies to wonder if you have gone crazy.

It can be done, and if you succeed, I guarantee you will have much more fun every day than you ever had before. You will have much more enthusiastic employees, which will no doubt affect your sales. Don't be surprised if—after some turbulence—your company's bottom line will skyrocket.

FOOD FOR THOUGHT

Think of your job as a manager:

What do you really think your company needs? A loyal manager who does her best to do everything in her job description? Or a manager who dares to think the unthinkable and create a new platform for innovation and growth?

Look upon the current design of your organization:

- Which elements are conventional first cycle design?
- Which elements are second cycle design?
- Are you motivated to take the next step?
- What is the order of magnitude of the gain you could get if everybody in your organization was liberated to do his best?
- What holds you back?
- What have you done to prepare the ground for a change?

6

Leadership

FIRST CYCLE MANAGEMENT

When a company is young and fast growing, few employees doubt why the company is successful. The company grows because it has hit the rare combination of dynamic entrepreneurs who have spotted a need in the market place, designed and delivered a solution, and managed the whole thing with great enthusiasm and focus on satisfying customer needs.

In this first phase or upward phase of the first cycle, values are normally absolutely clear, but seldom written down. The team just goes for it and if someone makes a mistake, it becomes highly visible and can be corrected quickly because the organization is small and management is hands-on.

When the company becomes larger and more established, the need grows for strategies, goals, and values in writing. At this point, consultants often come in and help management write numerous papers that end up as full-color glossy brochures. Here is an example of a set of values for a pharmaceutical company:

- *Imaginative—Dare to be different.*
  We are open-minded and resourceful with the courage to explore new ways to push the boundaries of treatment for CNS disorders.

- *Passionate—Never give up.*
  We believe actions speak louder than words, responding to change with energy and confidence. And we never give up.

- *Responsible—Do the right thing.*
  Our reputation is built on respect, trust, and integrity, and we understand that our decisions and actions can have a major impact on others.

Although these values are highly respectable, they are also very general and offer only limited guidance for employees in their daily work. Moreover, they are weak in the sense that they express 90 percent of what every company in the industry would do. You can check this by negating each of the three points:

- *Not imaginative—Not daring to be different.*
  We are neither open-minded nor resourceful, and we lack the courage to explore new ways to push the boundaries of treatment for CNS disorders.

- *Not passionate—We do give up.*
  We don't believe actions speak louder than words, and we respond to change without energy and confidence. And we do give up.

- *Irresponsible—Do the wrong thing.*
  Our reputation is not built on respect, trust, and integrity, and we do not understand that our decisions and actions can have a major impact on others.

The three values become meaningless if negated, which indicates that any other pharmaceutical company would most likely subscribe to the same values as the company in question. Therefore, the values aren't of much use to guide employee behavior. They are classical late-stage first cycle values.

Take a look at your own organization's values. Are they written down or are they communicated in another way? Try to negate them—that is, try to express the opposite. Is that meaningful or is it an empty statement that almost goes without saying? If the opposite makes a meaningful point (which you will most likely disagree with), the value statement has value.

VALUE BASED OR POWER BASED?

There is a case for limiting values to generalities that really don't say much. Such values leave maximum freedom for management to do what it wants.

Look at world-leading tool management company, Unimerco. Part of its value system is this sentence:

> **Unimerco** does not consider lay offs as a means to protect our bottom line.

Almost all companies seem to subscribe to the opposite principle if you follow how they respond to investor pressure for downsizing and outsourcing, but Unimerco doesn't. If the business faces a downturn, Unimerco seeks other ways to protect its bottom line. It may ask employees to reduce working hours or reduce salaries. It may ask employees to work longer without extra pay, or it may simply suffer a loss in the period it takes to adjust to the difficult business conditions.

That value statement is very powerful, because it binds management to behave in a certain manner. Unimerco has stuck to this principle for many years, and every time tough times have arisen, Unimerco has managed. The result is an unmatched loyalty and team spirit from all staff. Who would not go through fire and water for a company like that?

How can you describe your values in a way that is easy to understand for all staff? How can you ensure that there is consensus about the values among management and staff? How can you translate values into behavior for both managers and staff?

In this chapter, you explore these issues in principle. You can find a hands-on guide for doing this in practice in Chapter 7, "The Toolbox."

The opposite of value-based leadership is power-based management. At Unimerco, management has given up part of its power (the right to fire people in order to protect the bottom line) by deciding to run the business based on values. This illustrates the two different mental models of value-based leadership and power-based management, which are summarized in Table 6-1.

Table 6-1 Power-Based Management Versus Value-Based Leadership

	Power-Based Management	Value-Based Leadership
How values emerge	Values are defined by management and may be explicit or implicit.	Values are defined through a dialog between management and staff, and they are explicit.
How values are communicated	Values are contained in broad mission statements. Implicit values become known through actual management behavior.	Values get known through the definition process and through management's ongoing communication about the thinking behind concrete actions.
How values are implemented	By management through corporate communication and concrete action.	By management through a consensus building process with staff. Staff is urged to constantly monitor management behavior in order to spot examples of value and behavior inconsistence.
What's in it for staff?	Staff knows what is important or acceptable in the organization.	Staff knows that there is consistency between management behavior and official values. However, there is a psychological contract, which obliges staff to meet the organization's expectations.

You may wonder why values are featured in both columns: power-based management and value-based leadership. This is no mistake because values are present in all forms of management, also conventional power-based management.

EVERY ORGANIZATION HAS VALUES

Think of conventional CEOs in manufacturing operations. They normally do not talk about values. They likely *behave* in a way that clearly indicates that they have values, however. For instance, they have probably put in place an efficient system for controlling that every employee puts in the agreed number of working hours. They need such a system for practical purposes—for example, to calculate wages and follow up on production costs per department. But they also want it to control employees, because they don't trust them. One of their fundamental values is mistrust: If workers were not controlled, they would work less hours and they would most likely also steal whatever they needed from the factory. Of course, there are exceptions to this picture, but the majority of factory managers behave as though they have very clear values in this direction.

This is not limited to factory managers. Think of conventional CEOs. They protect their computers, their files, and their office from theft of information and equipment. Do they trust their fellow staff members? Do they believe in transparency? Think of the experienced salesperson who does not share her tricks with her colleagues because she wants to stay number one in the sales competition. Does she have values?

What would the answers to the preceding questions be in your own organization?

The key point is that all companies and all managers have values. The difference between power-based management and value-based leadership is whether these values are taken seriously, written down, and open for discussion.

To practice value-based leadership starts by writing down the values that you as a CEO intend to follow. Next, you share these values with your colleagues and modify them if needed. After the management team has reached consensus, you perform a reality check: Do we practice what we preach? If not, there is a need to change practice and then share the values with the staff—all staff. Not by lecturing about company values and their importance, but by inviting every employee to join into a dialogue about the values. In all, these values may need to be modified to be understood and accepted by all involved.

VALUES THAT MAKE A DIFFERENCE

Many managers lack a language to speak about values. They gladly lecture about top line growth, contribution margins, investments, and cash flow, but when it comes to values, they often don't know what to say. They lack the proper language.

You may be helped by this very simple structure, which builds on three elements:

- *Assumptions* about staff, their wishes and aspirations. Assumptions may be true or false in each individual case, but from the company's point of view, they are a choice. They represent the values that the company has decided to build on.
  Example: We assume that every employee in this organization fundamentally wants to do her best for the benefit of the company.

- *Norms* that express how the company implements the assumptions—that is, which consequences the management has decided should follow from the assumptions.
  Example: Therefore, we will make every effort to help each employee to contribute as much as possible to the company, and we will spend little or no time to control whether employees contribute the minimum working hours and other obligations that follow from their contract with the company.

- *Obligations* for employees that follow from the norms.
  Example: Therefore, we expect that every single employee strives to do his best to make the maximum contribution to the company.

The preceding may sound somewhat theoretical at first glance, but when you see how this is done in practice (see Chapter 7), you will realize that it is not theoretical at all. It is actually a most powerful management idea. In Chapter 7, you can find a write-up of the nine core values of Oticon, how they were implemented, and what that meant for employees.

Power-based management does not invite objections and complaints. Value-based leadership does. In any organization, there are managers that don't follow the rules in day-to-day management. Most often, the CEO never gets informed. However, if the rules have been established by consensus, and there is a paper that describes the assumptions, the norms, and the obligations in detail, employees do not hesitate to bring up cases of misbehavior. They know that top management takes the values seriously, and they know that bringing up examples of situations where the company does not practice what it preaches is a help, not troublemaking.

This has two positive effects: It prevents most misbehavior, and it brings any problems to the attention of top management for action. You will be surprised how such peer feedback can streamline the management of even a large organization. And even better: Clear values, norms, and obligations help eliminate the need for management. Employees know exactly what they can expect and what the company expects from them.

 Think for a moment of your own organization. Write down your own basic beliefs (assumptions) and those beliefs of the current management (if that is not you). Keep your notes for Chapter 7's section, "Value Identification Process."

THE ROLE OF MIDDLE MANAGEMENT

In virtually every successful turnaround management case, the issue of middle management involvement comes up. Middle management is almost never an engine that stimulates change. Middle management is an insulation layer or a filter layer that prevents management from carrying through the changes that need to be made.

How does middle management fit into the second cycle?

In the organic, nonhierarchical organization of second cycle organizations, there is no need for middle management in the conventional sense—that is, control and supervision of employees to ensure that they work hard and stay focused. However, there is a great need for the following:

- Mentors who can inspire, stimulate, and support employees to do their best and constantly develop as human beings in the organization.

- Project leaders who can form and lead a team to execute a task quickly, efficiently, innovatively, and reliably.

- Professional coordinators (or gurus) who master one or more professions, guide employees to perform high-quality professional work, and develop the profession to world-class level.

- Specialists who can get the work done as members of project teams.

- Process designers who can continuously improve business and learning processes of the organization.

The role of middle managers in the first cycle has been hands-on line management of a department—that is, a group of employees. The core of the second cycle collaborative organization is that employees manage themselves. Therefore, middle managers are needed for a different and wider variety of roles in the second cycle.

Most middle managers are promoted to their positions because they are the best specialists in the organization. In many cases, the promotion results in the loss of an excellent specialist and the gain of a bad manager. This fact comes from the observation that specialists are often introverted and highly fact based and rational, whereas good leaders are often more extroverted and emotion and idea based.

The change of roles for middle managers is often difficult, but when implemented, most former middle managers agree that they create more value to the company and are happier as human beings than before.

 Are you a middle manager yourself? How were you promoted? Were you the best specialist (or professional) around? If you were free to choose, which of the roles would you prefer? Mentor, project leader, guru, specialist, or process designer?

THE SECOND CYCLE PLATFORM

Value-based leadership comprises the fourth and final element of the second cycle platform:

- A *meaning* that goes beyond making money
- *Partnership* with staff and *networking* with suppliers, customers, and other external parties
- *Collaborative* organization
- Value-based *leadership*

The four elements are highly interdependent, and the platform for the second cycle is unlikely to work if all four elements are not present.

If a *meaning* beyond making money is lacking—that is, if the overall goal of the organization is to make money for shareholders—it is difficult to establish a real partnership between the company and its employees. Employees rightly ask themselves what the motivation is to partner with a company that only has one point on the agenda: to make as much money as possible for the owners based on our work. The same goes for external parties. Suppliers ask themselves what the motivation is to partner with a company that thinks short-term shareholder value will always buy at the lowest possible price and never live up a long-term strategic partnership.

Meaning is the key to operate an organic nonhierarchical organizational structure because lack of hierarchy requires all employees to think for themselves at how they can best contribute to the fundamental meaning of the company. There are no managers to tell them what to do.

If there is a meaning in the company, but management cannot establish a genuine *partnership* with employees, the spaghetti organization won't work. The same goes for *value-based leadership*. It is the value system that allows organization to work organically without constant problems with employee behavior. And value-based leadership becomes almost meaningless if there is not a common direction (or meaning) for everything the organization does.

In other words, the spaghetti organization is the engine, which can provide the power for the second cycle to take off and continue. The meaning and the values are the direction to go and the traffic rules to follow, whereas the partnership is the motivation for all involved to join in the journey.

The bottom line: Value-based leadership in a collaborative organization that is networked with external partners and builds on a partnership between all involved with a common direction or meaning can eliminate 80 percent or more of the need for day-to-day management. Imagine all the top specialists and great project managers that need not perform traditional day-to-day management any more. They are now ready to add value to customers through better products, more efficient supply chain design, better service, better marketing, and better dialog. You are ready to break the first cycle and enter the second cycle!

Now you know where to go, but you may not have the right equipment for the journey. Most of what you need is in my toolbox. May I invite you to take a look?

FOOD FOR THOUGHT

Think of your organization today:

- Which parts of its management practice are power-based and which parts are value-based?
- What are the official values and where are they written down?
- What are the real values as you see them?
- Does management invite discussion about the values?
- How do the official values conform to the behavior of management and employees?
- What prevents the organization from being value-based?

7

The Toolbox

TAKE A LOOK INTO MY PRIVATE TOOLBOX

Having read the previous chapters, you should now be ready to look at some hands-on tools that you can use to refresh your organization and help get it out of the lifecycle trap.

That's what this chapter is about. It offers you a selection of tools developed to overcome some of the most critical obstacles in the process of changing conventional organizations into high-performance innovative ones that can avoid the lifecycle trap.

Most of what you find in the toolbox is homemade. Tools have been inspired by others, of course, but I have adapted each tool to the particular purpose of revitalizing mature organizations. Each tool was designed and crafted from pure necessity. Here are the rubber boots you need when the road becomes really muddy.

The toolbox contains seven main tools in four departments, as listed in Table 7-1.

Table 7-1 Seven Important Tools

Department	Tool	Application
Assessment	TSC (break the cycle) index	A rough assessment tool to help you find out if your organization is infected by the lifecycle disease.
	MMM (mental model mapper)	A guide to analyze current mental models and develop alternative ones.
Establish the foundation	VIP (value identification process)	A process to help you identify the values of your organization and turn them into reality.
	CCCP (consensus creation crash process)	A process to help you create a consensus in your organization about values and their implementation.
Running the show	KPM (knowledge-based people management)	A set of tools to ensure that you utilize staff resources to the maximum extent.
	IP (innovation powerhouse)	A set of ideas to turn the workplace into an innovation powerhouse.
Transformation	CPT (change process tools)	A set of tools and ideas to move the organization from conventional habits into innovative and flexible behavior.

All the preceding tools have worked well in different situations, and there is a good chance they will work for you. However, success depends not only on good tools—the craftsman is essential.

THE BREAK THE CYCLE (BTC) INDEX

Oticon and other organizations caught in the first cycle trap have many common characteristics. In general, they lack a genuine meaning beyond making money for shareholders. They fail when the obituary test is applied to them. They do not see their employees, their suppliers, and their customers as partners, and they consider their relationships with these three groups as zero-sum games rather than win-win games. They suffer from a rigid internal structure with too many management layers and Chinese walls between departments. Their job designs are narrow and inflexible, and communication is formalized. They often work in nice premises, but the physical design of their workplaces prevents informal interaction between staff, particularly staff from different departments. Managers hide in their offices and believe in budgets and strategic plans as a religion for success.

The opposite, surprisingly enough, seems to be true in other companies I worked for or studied. Organizations that are opposite these characteristics seem to enjoy a more sustainable success. They are better able to sense changes in the market place and react quicker to the challenges. They act rather than react, and they change their priorities and behavior much quicker and with much less resistance from their organizations.

The research carried out so far does not guarantee that there is a one-to-one relationship between companies that enjoy sustainable success and companies that meet the four break the cycle (BTC) criteria that have been described in this book. Two decades of management experience in different industries and different parts of the world strongly indicate that there is a quite strong relationship between organizations that are innovative, flexible, and energetic, and those that have meaning, practice partnership, organize themselves the "spaghetti way," and are lead by people who are driven by values more than budgets—that is, follow the BTC criteria.

In this section, you find a small tool that may help you and your organization find out to what extent you are caught in the cycle— that is, to what extent your organization fulfills or doesn't fulfill the BTC criteria: meaning, partnership, collaboration, and value-based leadership. Through 60 questions that you and your staff members answer in less than 15 minutes, you can rate your organization on 10 dimensions that add up to the four aspects that characterize an organization that is (or isn't) caught in the cycle.

Averaging over the 10 dimensions, the outcome of the assessment is expressed in a BTC index, which ranges between 0 and 100. The tool is only a rough guideline, so small differences in scores are not important. As a rule of thumb, scores should be interpreted in three main categories only, as described in Table 7-2.

Table 7-2 Interpreting Your BTC Index

BTC index	Color	Interpretation
60–100	Green	The organization is most likely well prepared for the challenges ahead. However, there may be room for improvement on certain aspects.
40–60	Yellow	The organization most likely has some weaknesses that should be addressed to avoid the lifecycle trap.
00–40	Red	The organization most likely cannot meet the challenges that lie ahead. It needs to reconsider its mental model and be prepared for fundamental changes.

Although the BTC index tool has been limited to a rough overall assessment, it is relevant to look at the individual scores for each of the 10 underlying dimensions. Table 7-3 indicates how individual scores should be interpreted.

Table 7-3 Interpreting Individual BTC Scores

BTC criterion	BTC dimension	High score	Low score
Meaning	Customer focus	Customers have highest priority and the organization is responsive to customer needs.	Internal matters win over customer needs or the organization seems to rely more upon its own ideas than actual customer needs.
	Stakeholder orientation	Needs of customers, employees, and other stakeholders are balanced against pure shareholder returns.	Short-term profit and focus is more important than balancing the needs of different shareholders.
Partnership	Internal partnership orientation	Management and employees consider themselves to be in the same boat.	Management and employees consider themselves two different groups that do not always have the same goals.
Networking	External partnership orientation	The organization maintains long-term relationships with suppliers and customers, most likely playing a win-win game.	Suppliers and customers are treated at an arms-length basis to maintain the strongest possible bargaining position.

BTC criterion	BTC dimension	High score	Low score
Collaborative organization	Non-rigid internal structure	The organization adapts its structures to actual challenges and involves employees in decision-making if they have relevant knowledge.	The hierarchy is important and the organization works within the framework of a rigid organizational structure.
	Flexible job design and teamwork	Jobs tend to develop with the person that has the job. Individuals perceive only few limitations in performing their jobs.	Jobs are well-defined and relatively constant over time. Each individual employee is supposed to do the job and not too much more.
	Informal and direct communication	Communication is informal and direct—that is, not limited by departmental barriers or organizational levels.	Communication is more formal and the company encourages the use of the correct line of command—that is, most coordination between departments is handled by management.
	Creative and flexible workplace	The workplace is open, flexible, and stimulating.	The workplace is structured and reflects the organizational structures of the organization.
Value-based leadership	Leadership	Managers interact with staff and focus on setting goals and overall direction rather than managing details.	Management is less visible and focuses on making the right decisions and making sure they are implemented correctly.
	Value-orientation	Managers are guided by a set of values and fundamentally trust employees as partners.	Managers define tasks for individual employees and follow up on them to ensure that the work is done properly.
BTC index	*Overall assessment*	The organization is flexible, responsive, networked, and innovative.	The organization is rigid, maybe arrogant, rather self-contained, and often traditional.

The BTC index assessment tool may be used in two different ways:

- You as an individual may use the self-assessment tool to clarify and quantify your own impression of the organization's position. Do you think your organization in danger of being caught in the cycle?

- As a manager or HR professional, you may use the self-assessment tool on a company-wide or division-wide basis to pool the input from all staff on the matter. Does the input from your employees indicate that your organization might be caught in the cycle?

The BTC self-assessment tool is available for you and other readers of this book. You may perform an individual or company-wide assessment by visiting www.thesecondcycle.com.

Most likely, you will want to take the self-assessment first and then set one up for all employees in your department, division, or the entire organization.

After you do either an individual or a company-wide assessment, bear in mind that top managers (or people close to top management) tend to assess the situation more positively than most employees. Managers seem less limited by hierarchies the higher they are placed in them. They perceive that they have more freedom to take initiatives and cross barriers, and they don't sense a culture of control to the same extent as their subordinates. So, if you as a manager of an organization score a BTC index for your organization of 75 or more, it doesn't necessarily mean that everything is fine. Before making your conclusion, let your staff at different levels do the assessment, and most likely you are in for a great surprise! Perhaps not a pleasant one!

MENTAL MODEL MAPPER

While working with revitalization of a mature organization, you need a system or a procedure that can help you quickly analyze a company's thinking, how it got there, and where it can go alternatively. You may also need this system if you are asked to join a company's board of directors or when you consider buying shares in a business. You also benefit from it before you enter into negotiations with a business for some reason.

Fortunately, this is by no means rocket science—just a framework to ask questions in a systematic fashion and put the answers together into a comprehensive picture. That's what the mental model mapper is about.

Go through the following process assuming you are looking at someone else's company. Do this before you go through the process for your own company or organization. If you start with your own organization, you may easily be blinded, which makes it difficult to be objective. Having done a few analyses of other companies first makes it easier for you to analyze your own.

Start the process by getting to know as much as possible about the businesses in question. Study their websites and annual reports; look at their brochures and advertisements; note how they work through different sales channels; look at how they have organized their supply chain; speak to employees, customers, and other people that are affected by the firm; and try to understand how they look upon their main stakeholders including local community and the environment.

From there, you go through five easy steps:

1. Map the current mental model for each key aspect of the company. Summarize the mental model in a short statement of the company's current overall idea.

2. If possible, find out where each aspect of that mental model came from. What was its origin and why was it chosen?

3. Take a hard look at the origin. Is the situation still valid or relevant today? What has changed?

4. Imagine that you were to design a new mental model based on the situation today (and how you expect it to be tomorrow). What would that mental model look like for each of the key aspects? Summarize the new mental model into an overall idea.

5. Compare Steps 1 and 4 and conclude.

STEP 1: MAP THE CURRENT MENTAL MODEL

Assume you have the basic information and start systematically mapping the company's current mental model by key aspect. Table 7-4 shows Oticon's view of its customers prior to the transformation of the company.

Table 7-4 Mapping Oticon's Mental Model in the Behind-the-Ear Period.

Key aspect	Current mental model—that is, how the organization looks upon itself today
Customers	Oticon viewed the audiologists as its customers. Oticon perceived the audiologists as professionals that had an almost scientific approach to their work. Audiologists were assumed to be able to understand and appreciate technological advances. Oticon assumed that audiologists measured successful hearing aid fittings by comparing actual amplification with a calculated target based on state-of-the art theory.
End users	
Intermediates	
Other aspects of the selling process	
Suppliers	
Product	
Criterion for success	
Employees	
Organization	
Physical environment	
Technology	
Supply chain	
Other aspects	

One company may look upon customers as the end users of its product, whereas another company in the same industry may see the intermediate (for example, the retail shop) as its customer. Companies may consider their customers as partners with a common goal, whereas others may see customers as opposites that they exploit to the maximum extent. In the hearing aid industry, some companies looked upon the end user as a patient, whereas others saw the user as a customer. In the car industry, some companies view customers as environmentally conscious if they are given the chance to buy an environmentally friendly car, whereas others simply look at the outcome of market research where customers express their preferences for comfort, safety, speed, design, and so on. Mental models vary significantly within the same industry.

For each key aspect, you need to map how you believe the company looks upon itself. Some aspects may not be valid for some companies, whereas other companies or organizations have special aspects that are not on the list. Keep flexible and omit all aspects that do not contain important information. Keep it simple!

In the preceding example, Oticon had a very specific mental model of its perceived customers. Some competitors also assumed that audiologists were their customers, but they viewed audiologists less as scientists (as Oticon did) and more as businesspeople. Still other competitors in the industry focused on the end users as their customers and saw audiologists only as intermediaries.

After you have mapped the current mental model, you need to summarize your findings into an overall idea for the business you are looking at.

Oticon's overall idea in the behind-the-ears days might be summarized as follows:

> Oticon is a research-based company that aims to design, manufacture, and sell the world's most advanced and reliable hearing aids. We work through qualified audiologists to achieve the best possible treatment of hearing loss.

After you believe you understand the company's current mental model, you are ready to move on.

STEP 2: TRACE THE ORIGIN OF THE MENTAL MODEL

Before proposing alternatives, it is useful to force oneself to look back and find out where the current mental model came from. In most cases, there is a historical explanation.

Imagine you were performing this analysis at the peak of Oticon's success with behind-the-ear hearing aids. Oticon was focused on audiologists. That was because Oticon's main product—the behind-the-ear hearing aid—was pushed very strongly by audiologists that demanded the previous generation of pocket hearing aids to be substituted by hearing aids that were placed at the ear only. Those audiologists were scientifically oriented. They demanded linear frequency response, high signal-to-noise ratios, wide adjustment ranges, and high reliability. They were the most demanding and trend-setting customers in the world.

With that information, it is not difficult to understand why Oticon was obsessed with fulfilling the audiologists' needs. Oticon perceived end users as customers of the audiologists, not of Oticon. Oticon maintained a scientific focus on end users and obviously involved end users in field tests and other research. But it was the role of audiologists to express the needs of users—not Oticon's role.

Such historical explanations can be found for most companies. There are good reasons for their choice of mental models. Step 2 of the process is to find the origin of each aspect of the mental model as far as possible.

The result of this analysis is placed in a new column in Table 7-5.

Table 7-5 Mapping the Origin of Oticon's Mental Model

Key aspect	Current mental model—that is, how the organization looks upon itself today	Origin of current mental model
Customers Example: Oticon in the behind-the-ear days	Audiologists are customers that take care of patients. Audiologists look for advanced technology. Their approach is scientific.	Audiologists drove product innovation in the 1960s by demanding acoustical performance and reliability.

You need to trace the origin of every key aspect of the current mental model before moving to the next phase.

STEP 3: IS THE SITUATION AT ORIGIN STILL VALID?

Having traced the origin of the current mental model, you need to assess whether the situation that was the source of the current mental model at that point in time is still valid today.

You need to add another column to the table to record the results. Look at the Oticon behind-the-ear case shown in Table 7-6.

Table 7-6 Validating the Origin of Oticon's Mental Model

Key aspect	Current mental model—that is, how the organization looks upon itself today	Origin of current mental model	Is the situation at origin still valid?
Customers Example: Oticon in the behind-the-ear days	Audiologists are customers that take care of patients. Audiologists look for advanced technology. Their approach is scientific.	Audiologists drove product innovation in the 1960s by demanding acoustical performance and reliability.	Twenty years later, end users no longer saw themselves as patients. They became consumers, and they started to play a much more important role in the choice of hearing aid.

The situation changed dramatically: End users jumped out of the patient role and saw themselves as consumers. They gradually became younger and were asked to pay all or part of the hearing aid themselves.

That change added invisibility—in addition to acoustical performance—as a key demand parameter. However, Oticon's mental model remained unchanged.

So, the challenge in Step 3 is to assess if the basis for originally choosing each key aspect of the current mental model is still valid. This serves as a great inspiration to imagine different mental models.

STEP 4: DESIGN ONE OR MORE NEW MENTAL MODELS

You will be surprised how many examples you can find of well-established organizations that apply mental models that build on assumptions that are outdated today.

To design a new mental model, you should add one last column to the table to contain aspects of a possible new mental model for the organization (see Table 7-7).

Table 7-7 Possible Alternatives to Oticon's Mental Model

Key aspect	Current mental model—that is, how the organization looks upon itself today	Origin of current mental model	Is the situation at origin still valid?	Possible new mental models
Customers Example: Oticon in the behind-the-ear days	Audiologists are customers that take care of patients. Audiologists look for advanced technology. Their approach is scientific.	Audiologists drove product innovation in the 1960s by demanding acoustical performance and reliability.	Twenty years later, end users no longer saw themselves as patients. They became consumers, and they started to play a much more important role in the choice of hearing aid.	Join forces with audiologists to achieve maximum end user delight. Focus on the entire customer experience and fine-tune each step to add value and form a pleasant user experience. Balance cosmetics and acoustical performance.

Although we did not know what a mental model was at that time, this was the process we went through at Oticon to challenge our own assumptions about customers, intermediaries, products, employees, organization, and physical workplace. We made the audiologist a partner instead of just a customer, and we redefined our reason from "developing, manufacturing, and selling the world's best hearing aids" to "help[ing] people with impaired hearing live as they wish with the hearing they have."

Having identified possible new mental models for each key aspect, you need to summarize your findings into an overall idea just like you did when you mapped the current mental model.

STEP 5: COMPARING CURRENT AND NEW MENTAL MODELS

The comparison is essential to highlight the key changes and their reasons. Most likely, this leads you to review each step in the process to refine your arguments and sharpen your conclusion.

Take a while to perform this analysis—first, on one or two organizations that you know (without being part of them) and second, on your own organization. You may be in for a surprise!

In Chapter 8, "What If They Broke the Cycle: Three Live Case Studies," you will find some examples of this analysis. You don't need to be an industry expert to do this analysis, but be prepared. Established companies will challenge your analysis. How can an outsider dream of telling large and well-established institutions that they are completely off on key aspects of their business?

If in trouble, summarize the main points in Hans Christian Andersen's fairy tale about the emperor's new clothes.

VALUE IDENTIFICATION PROCESS (VIP)

If you hired an MBA, you would expect her to be able to distinguish between fixed and variable costs, profit and cash flow, and assets and liabilities. You would expect the MBA to understand the basics of marketing and strategy, and you would be surprised if she could not analyze your company's supply chain and proposed improvements to it.

Would you also expect your MBA to be able to establish a value system for your company and link it to management and staff behavior?

You should expect it, because value-based leadership is the only sustainable way to manage tomorrow's knowledge-based and highly innovative organizations. But you probably won't find it, because many managers lack a language to speak about values. They may feel that values are important, but they often don't know how to speak about values in a consistent and precise way.

To do so, you can apply a very simple structure, which builds on three elements:

- *Assumptions* about staff, their wishes, and their aspirations. Assumptions may be true or false in each individual case, but from the company's point of view, they are a choice.

- *Norms* that express how the company implements the assumptions—that is, which consequences the management thinks should follow from the assumptions.
- *Obligations* for employees that follow from the norms.

The process is quite simple: It starts with the head of the organization—the CEO, chairman, or managing director. If you are not the privileged holder of such a job, you should do the work anyway. One day, you might end up having the job!

First, think about your own fundamental values—that is, assumptions about people. Be honest in this phase. Later, you may have to change your mind or quit as a CEO; but at this point, you should be absolutely honest.

Start looking at one tough question:

> How do you think your employees want to be treated by management? Do they want to take responsibility if you grant them opportunities to do so? Or do they want management to take responsibility while the employees simply do what they are told?

Let's assume that you honestly think your employees don't want to take responsibility. In that case, there are two possibilities: Either you are right, or you are wrong. If you are right, you have a problem. Because you cannot run the type of knowledge-based, responsive, and highly innovative organization that this book is about if your employees are not willing to take responsibility.

In principle, you should fire everyone and find responsible people for your organization. Before firing your employees, however, you might want to perform a reality check. Most likely, you will be surprised and find that most employees actually want to take responsibility if management treats them as partners rather than opposites. It may be your behavior that leads your employees to act in a way that is not responsible.

Whether you are right or wrong, you have to make a decision: On which assumption do you want to run the company? I don't think there is much of a choice, but it may be that you think your industry is very special and requires a very directive approach. Make up your mind and think of which management behavior actually reflects the assumption you chose.

Be aware that we discuss assumptions, not facts. The assumptions are what you choose to build the company on. There will always be employees that do not conform to your assumptions, and if they continue to do so and you can't change the situation, they will eventually have to go.

Continuing the preceding example, we will look at two opposite assumptions and their consequences (see Table 7-8).

Table 7-8 Assumptions and How They Are Implemented (Norms)

Management assumption	Norms—that is, management behavior that reflects the chosen assumption
Every employee in this organization fundamentally *wants to take responsibility* if invited to do so.	Discuss company mission, vision, and goals with employees so that they may use their creativity to work smarter in that direction.
	Do everything to provide the best possible framework for employees to do an excellent job.
	Spend as few resources on control as possible.
	Let each employee decide as far as possible when, where, and how he wants to do the work.
Every employee in this organization fundamentally wants to *avoid taking responsibility*, even if invited to do so.	Communicate concrete goals and timelines to each employee so that she knows what to do, how to do it, and when.
	Make sure each employee knows exactly how you want the job done. Give detailed and specific instructions and document that you have done so.
	Follow up in detail on the progress of the work and take corrective action if the work does not progress as planned.

Now comes a moment of truth. Which assumption do you choose?

 Imagine you choose the first one: You assume that your staff wants to take responsibility. Then, you need to assess if the behavior of your organization actually matches that assumption. It probably doesn't match fully.

For example, look at the resources you spend on control: time clocks and elaborate overtime pay systems, and restrictions on the possibilities of your employees to spend company money. You may have requisition forms that request a "responsible person" (a manager) to sign off on even small purchases. Detailed procedures for approving company travel and travel expenses.

Does this reflect the principle of spending minimum resources on control? Does this contribute to the best possible framework for employees to do an excellent job?

At this point, you might give up and choose the other assumption: Your staff wants to avoid taking responsibility. You could leave the time clocks where they are and maintain the restrictions on company spending and company travel. But you would not develop the fast-moving, responsive, and highly innovative organization that is likely to be tomorrow's winner.

Next, you have to start adapting real-life of the organization to your assumptions. You need to change rules and procedures. You need to discuss the issue with middle management and employee representatives and gain their acceptance and commitment. How you do this is the subject of the consensus building crash tool in the next section. Imagine that you have managed to align the behavior of the organization with the assumptions you have chosen to base the company on. You have reached consensus among managers and employees that the assumptions (values) are fair and acceptable, and you have gained acceptance from employees that management has done its job by aligning day-to-day behavior with the company values.

If you have aligned management's assumptions with day-to-day behavior, you have created a platform for a new and very strong relationship with employees: the psychological contract.

The psychological contract is the link between how you run your organization and how employees behave. You will see that if management has written down the values (assumptions) and practices what it preaches, employees will accept the values and be willing to contribute their part of the equation. For example, if management assumes that employees are responsible adults and treats employees as such, the vast majority of employees will behave responsibly.

Take a look at the example once again in Table 7-9.

Table 7-9 Assumptions and Norms and What They Mean for Employees

Management assumption	Norms—that is, management behavior that reflects the chosen assumption	Employee obligations that reflect values (management assumptions) and norms
Every employee in this organization fundamentally *wants to take responsibility* if invited to do so.	Discuss company mission, vision, and goals with employees so that they may use their creativity to work smarter in that direction.	Participate actively in discussions on company mission and such and take initiatives by proposing new ways to get there.
	Do everything we can to provide the best possible framework for employees to do an excellent job.	Make every effort to do an excellent job.
	Spend as few resources on control as possible.	Live up to responsible behavior and do not misuse the confidence that the company shows in you.
	Let each employee decide as far as possible when, where, and how he wants to do the work.	Work efficiently, work hard, be flexible, and be responsible when you plan your work.

This is the tool you need to align the interests and the behavior of the company and its employees. If you can establish such a psychological contract, you will develop a teamwork that is very difficult to beat. This teamwork is a great advantage for the company, but not only for the company. Employees like to be part of the show. They appreciate that the company is open about its values. They want to be part of a consensus building process.

Is this realistic? Yes, it is, not only in Scandinavia, but everywhere. The obstacle is not employees; it is management. Even in countries where there is traditionally a very long distance between management and employees (distance of power), which normally leads to lack of employee responsibility, it can be done. Everybody wants to be an associate rather than a slave.

The key is to create that consensus among managers and between management and employees. The consensus creation crash process in the next section is designed to do exactly that.

Before moving there, we need to expand the values, norms, and obligations to all important aspects of the day-to-day functioning of the organization. At Oticon, where we went through this process as part of the transformation into a truly knowledge-based organization, we chose the following eight aspects:

- *Responsibility.* Described previously.

- *Development.* That is, the opportunity and obligation for employees to constantly improve their competencies.

- *Freedom.* That is, the ability to have maximum freedom at work and the obligations that follow.

- *Understanding.* That is, the need to understand one's own job and how it links to the work of other people.

- *Growth.* That is, the wish to be part of a company that develops and grows constantly and the need to play an active part in the process.

- *Partnership.* That is, the need to act as partners for a common goal instead of opposites performing a zero-sum game.

- *Feedback.* That is, the obligation to provide honest feedback and reward employees in a fair manner.

- *Security.* That is, the need for employees to have job security and the obligation to constantly qualify for it.

You can see how company values about these eight aspects of work were translated into norms (management behavior) and obligations when we went through this process at Oticon as part of the transformation in the beginning of the 1990s (see Table 7-10). The company has constantly modified and developed these points to fit changing realities.

VALUES, NORMS, AND OBLIGATIONS

AN EXAMPLE FROM OTICON

As you are aware, the Oticon transformation that is described in Chapter 1, "The First Cycle: Why Success Breeds Failure," was a fundamental change of culture from a traditional hierarchical line-staff organization into a fast-moving flexible, responsive, and highly innovative organization. That could not have been done without defining a set of common values, creating a consensus among all involved, and aligning the entire operation to reflect those values. Table 7-10 shows Oticon's values (assumptions), norms, and obligations as they were about five years after the transformation had taken place. At that time, the values and all that went with them had gone through two revisions.

Table 7-10 Oticon's Assumptions, Norms, and Expectations Versus Employees

Responsibility

Management assumptions:	How we implement them:	Expectations:
Oticon employees want to be treated as independent individuals who are willing to take responsibility when the opportunity arises.	We focus on agreeing goals and frameworks, and trust the employees to plan and carry out tasks themselves. We spend the least possible time on control. Wherever possible, it is the employees who determine their tasks, working hours, and workstation location.	Employees are willing to assume responsibility for planning and implementing tasks themselves. Employees behave responsibly and are willing to make decisions even at the risk of making mistakes. We accept that mistakes can happen, but expect staff to learn from them and ensure that they are not repeated.

Development

Management assumptions:	How we implement them:	Expectations:
Oticon employees want to develop within their jobs and gain new experience within the company. Exciting and challenging tasks are more important than formal status and titles.	We make it possible for employees to assume several tasks at the same time, if they are interested and capable of doing so. We want to avoid confining employees within narrow professional boundaries. By abolishing hierarchical departmental structures, we make it easy for employees to use any talent that lies beyond their own area of expertise. We have as few titles as possible and no formal career planning.	Employees take the initiative to explore other areas of capability that lie outside their own professional area. Employees accept an organization that is without formal status and titles, and forge their own careers by developing their expertise.

Freedom

Management assumptions:	How we implement them:	Expectations:
Oticon employees desire as much freedom as possible, yet accept the necessity of a clear and structured framework.	We have very few rules, preferring instead to encourage our employees to primarily use their common sense in their daily work.	Employees respect the few existing rules and honor agreements.

Understanding

Management assumptions:	How we implement them:	Expectations:
Oticon employees are eager to understand how their own tasks fit into the context of the whole company.	We create an open environment where employees have access to as much information as possible.	Employees seek out the information they need themselves. They show an active interest in the company as a whole in order to understand how their own work fits in.
	We strive to inform everyone about our strategies and business plans.	Employees treat all internal information confidentially, exercising care and discretion when passing on internal information.
	Being quoted on the Copenhagen Stock Exchange requires us to respect its rules of conduct, which limit the disclosure of certain information.	

Growth

Management assumptions:	How we implement them:	Expectations:
Oticon employees want to be part of a company that is continually developing.	We use time and resources on improving our way of working. We are open to new ideas and solutions.	Employees are open to new thinking and ready to adapt to change.

Partnership

Management assumptions:	How we implement them:	Expectations:
Oticon employees want to be treated as partners in the company.	The company's entire work structure reflects this notion.	Employees do their utmost to contribute to Oticon's growth and development.
		Employees are flexible and willing to make an extra effort when required—taking family and other duties into consideration.
		Employees share their knowledge with colleagues.

Feedback

Management assumptions:	How we implement them:	Expectations:
Oticon employees want varied, qualified feedback on their work and a salary corresponding to their contribution.	All levels of management should give honest and constructive feedback, whether positive or negative.	Employees are open-minded toward performance appraisals and are willing to invest in personal improvement.
	All employees participate in an annual performance appraisal with their mentor.	Employees give their managers honest feedback.
	Salaries are adjusted individually. The relevant people, project, and technical managers participate in evaluating the individual employee.	
	Evaluation is based on three factors: effort, the value of the work for Oticon, and market salary levels.	

Security

Management assumptions:	How we implement them:	Expectations:
Oticon employees want to feel secure in the working life.	We make it possible for staff to improve and develop their skills so that should they choose to move on, they have excellent prospects of finding work elsewhere. We provide financial support for continuous professional development.	Employees take their own initiative in developing their skills and are willing to attend courses in their spare time.

CONSENSUS CREATION CRASH PROGRAM (CCCP)

If you are a manager, you probably know everything worth knowing about your organization's customers and competition, the products and services, the cost structure, and the budget. You know which questions to ask to evaluate an investment, and you know the legislation and collective agreements about firing employees.

But do you know how to create consensus about ideas, values, and goals? Isn't that as important (or even more important) for any manager?

It is, but few managers know it anyway.

The consensus creation crash program (CCCP) is a tool you should try. It is simple to apply and no doubt will take you and your staff in the right direction. It may reveal problems that you did not know of; and if it does, you should be happy because realizing that you have a problem is the most important prerequisite for solving it.

The purpose of the CCCP is to push you, your management team, and your entire staff into consensus. You cannot be sure that consensus will emerge about regarding what you started with, but in most cases, it will come close, unless you were absolutely off from the beginning.

Let's assume you want to establish a consensus, first in the management team and later among all staff about the future value system and its interpretation in your organization (values, norms, and obligations). Table 7-11 shows the steps of the CCCP process.

Table 7-11 Main Steps in the CCCP Consensus Program

Phase	Step	Action
Management team preparation	Discuss and achieve preliminary conclusion.	Management team discusses and agrees upon values, norms, and obligations. Write down the conclusion in a format similar to the Oticon example. Be specific and as brief as possible. Allow for several discussion rounds.
Preparation	Prepare staff for dialog shop and invite.	Prepare and distribute the written statement that describes the values and their consequences. Invite everyone to read and raise issues at the upcoming dialog shop. Ask staff to be critical and look for a) inconsistency and b) examples where the values do not conform to reality.

Phase	Step	Action
Dialog shop	Introduce dialog shop	Assemble all participants and explain the process briefly. Highlight the need to find inconsistencies and examples of statements that do not conform to today's reality. Divide participants into groups of 10 to 25 persons so that each member of the management team can be allocated to a group. Invite each group to spend the first 15 minutes to prepare questions to management. Urge groups to be concrete and direct and to ask questions in a way that requires the manager to be specific. Prepare groups for the following dialogs in which they will have different managers. What about asking the same questions to different managers and looking for inconsistent answers?
	Prepare first dialog (15 minutes)	Each group prepares questions for the manager without knowing which manager it will get. If there is a climate of fear, groups may elect one person to ask all questions on behalf of the group. Normally, participants just ask the questions themselves.
	Dialog 1 (45 minutes)	Q&A session 1 with manager 1 (45 minutes). Group members take notes and write down ideas for additional questions in the later dialogs. Managers most likely come under severe pressure because many issues have not been sufficiently clarified in the preparatory phase.
	Digestion 1 (15 minutes)	15-minute break to digest answers and prepare additional questions in each group. At the same time, management team compares notes and prepares for rotation into groups. During this period, members of the management team may seek advice on answers to specific questions from other members of the management team. Members will also prepare the "next" person for difficult questions that may be expected in the next group.
	Dialog 2 (45 minutes)	Q&A session 2 with manager 2 (45 minutes). Managers continue to be under pressure because groups will sharpen questions. Managers are concerned if their answers might be inconsistent with what the previous manager said to the group. The good news is that the manager has tried it once before; he knows most of what to expect.
	Digestion 2 (15 minutes)	15-minute break to digest answers and prepare additional questions. Groups have most likely identified weak points and will focus further at these points. Management team compares notes in separate room and prepares for next rotation. At this point, managers start to regain control. Answers to more and more questions become "standard," and managers become better prepared for the following groups.

Phase	Step	Action
	Dialogs 3-6 (45 minutes each)	Q&A sessions 3, 4, 5, and 6 followed by breaks and ongoing rotation of management team. During these sessions, groups continue to dig deeper into key issues while management gradually improves performance by giving more and more consistent and clear answers to the critical questions. Groups get repeated explanations and gradually tend to understand and accept management's arguments (if they make sense).
	Digestion 3-6 (15 minutes each)	15-minute breaks to digest answers and prepare additional questions. Groups tend to understand and accept repeated answers (assuming they make sense). Managers get more and more relaxed because they have now clarified a number of issues that they had not discussed sufficiently during the preparation phase.
	Conclusion in plenary	Plenary session to highlight issues that need further attention. The head of the organization invites groups to bring forward any issues that they did not feel was answered to their satisfaction, typically because of inconsistencies. Normally, relatively few issues are brought up because groups have gotten multiple explanations from different managers that have become more and more consistent.
Followup	Revised paper	Management to address each issue that has been brought up. Management needs to take immediate action and inform about decisions and their implementation. Staff to be urged to bring up inconsistencies and other issues on an ongoing basis, first to the relevant manager and then to the head of the organization if the matter is not resolved.

You may argue that the process is dangerous. It may reveal that some members of the management team are not loyal to decisions, whereas others may not be able to withstand the pressure from the groups. That's actually good news because that gives the CEO an opportunity to see her team in action first-hand. If a manager is not up to speed, perhaps he should become a specialist. If a manager is not loyal, he and the CEO have something very relevant to talk about.

The process most likely also shows that some of the conclusions that you reached as a management team were not sufficiently clear or perhaps even wrong. Consensus emerges, but the subject matter for the consensus may have changed somewhat from where you started. Good news: The employees have had an influence, they have made a contribution, and you as a CEO can proudly say that your value system is a result of a joint effort from all involved—not only your thoughts.

The CCCP is a tool that is designed to help you and your team reach consensus. It was designed first of all to address soft issues, such as values and their implementation, but I have also used it to create consensus about hard points, such as strategy and direction.

Take a moment to reflect: Bearing in mind this is a very powerful tool, is the CCCP a fair process or is it a manipulation of both the employees and your leadership team?

I think the CCCP is fair. If employees disagree with the values you put forward, they can make their point and you will be forced to deal with the issue. If someone from your management team is inconsistent with the values and the rest of the team, he must comply or step down unless you change the values. That's much fairer than keeping managers that are disloyal to corporate values.

Another tool that I have used as a supplement to the dialog shop is the two-way meeting.

Most managers hold information meetings with their staff once per week, per month, or per quarter. Same procedure as last time: The boss tells about performance and issues and invites questions of which there are normally very few. Game over.

The two-way meeting is different. The managers simply make themselves available for a one-hour question-and-answer session. No introductory speech. Just make the team available for any question anyone might want to ask. The first time, there will be silence. One minute, two minutes, five minutes. Keep your mouth shut and enjoy the silence. Rest assured that you will not be sitting there for half an hour without anyone asking a single question. Someone will start, and others will follow. If you don't start with an introduction, you will find that the questions are very different from what you expected.

This is exactly the purpose of the session.

Apply this format about every third time you have an information meeting. Dialog will be greatly improved.

What do you think? Would you ever dare to just stand there in front of your employees and say nothing until somebody asks a question?

I think you should.

KNOWLEDGE-BASED PEOPLE MANAGEMENT (KPM)

You may wonder why I chose this title. Isn't people management always knowledge-based? I don't think so, because most people management or HRM (human resource management) is based on common sense and experience. It lacks genuine tools and systematic procedures to apply them. This is surprising because the issues that tend to come up in people management are the same over and over. People are different, but the issues are the same: recruiting, conflict resolution, team building, personal and management development, and the like.

This part of the toolbox aims to make people management more systematic and knowledge-based. No one can guarantee that you will stop making mistakes, even if you apply all the tools, but most likely, you will make fewer mistakes, which will benefit both your organization and the people in it.

People management mistakes are much more expensive than most people think. For example, take a sales department that has 10 salespeople on the road and 10 in-house backup staff. The people issue is to recruit a new sales manager for that department. Today's sales are about $20 million (U.S. dollars) and the contribution margin is 60 percent or $12 million. Budget indicates at least 10 percent sales growth next year. Imagine you hire a sales manager that isn't up to speed. He has shown excellent sales results personally, but he is not a team player. Two of your top salespeople quit, and motivation drops for the rest. In the first six months, sales drop 15 percent, and you realize that the person you employed has to go. Another six months until you have the successor in place.

What is the cost of that mistake?

Most people then think of the person's salary, let's say $120,000 for 12 months. But the actual loss is much larger: Annual sales did not grow by 10 percent; they dropped by 15 percent—that is, you lost $5 million in sales or $3 million in contribution. You lost two of your best salespeople. Such staff is very valuable if you look upon their sales over a number of years. The loss of the two may easily cost the company another $3 million in lost contribution over the coming years, plus the demotivation, the confusion, and the uncertainty, not to mention the customers lost to competition and the mistrust in management.

That easily adds up to a bill of not only the $120,000 annual salary, but rather $6 to $10 million, which is why people management is essential. If the risk of hiring the wrong person could be reduced from 20 percent to half of that, the gain would be something like $600,000 to $1 million in this single case. Knowledge-based HRM can have very high returns.

There are five main HR processes that you can improve dramatically by knowledge-based people management (see Table 7-12).

Table 7-12 Key Processes in Human Resource Management

HR process	Content
Recruiting	Profile job, profile ideal applicant, announce, screen applicants, profile short-list candidates, select candidate, fit candidate into organization, coach candidate and manager, follow up and learn from process.
Individual development	Profile employee, assess competencies and goals, prioritize, train and stimulate on-the-job development, follow up and learn from process.
Teambuilding	Profile team members; identify strengths, weaknesses, and potential conflicts in team; prioritize; train and stimulate on-the-task development; follow up and learn from process.
Management development	Profile manager including 360° view; identify strengths, weaknesses, and potential development goals; prioritize; train and stimulate on-the-job development; follow up and learn from process.
Organizational development	Profile organization; identify strengths, weaknesses, and potential development goals; prioritize; work with individual managers; repeat profile; follow up and learn from process.

The term *profile* occurs in every HR process in Table 7-12. Although I have a scientific background, I don't believe everything can be quantified in people management. The final selection of a candidate for a job should not be done by software expert systems. Rely on your intuition. But allow your intuition to be strongly influenced by facts before making a decision. Insist on having a profile of the job and how the job reflects in a profile of the ideal candidate. Compare short-list candidate profiles with the ideal profile, but do not always select the person whose profile fits the ideal best. Again, rely on your intuition: Do you fundamentally trust the candidate? Do you like her? Does she have an unusual background that makes you believe that she has a unique potential? Will she fit into your culture? Does she have a sense of humor?

There are many aspects of a person that cannot be included in the personal profile—even if it may come out of the world's best personal assessment system. That's where intuition comes in. But use it only after you have all the facts on the table.

Before moving on to each of the HR processes mentioned in Table 7-12, let's take a look at personal profiles that come out of personal assessment systems. Here is an example of a personal assessment profile that comes out of the system I have used most because it builds on C.G. Jung's psychological theory.

The profile includes four parts:

- *Fundamental factors.* Come out of Jung's theory as fundamental characteristics of the personality.
- *Inner driving forces.* That is, other factors that drive our behavior inside or outside the job situation. These factors are difficult to influence in the job situation.
- *Job-related factors.* That is, how we behave in the job in relation to other people.
- *Personal focus areas.* Cover aspects of our behavior that can most easily be influenced by the social setting of the job.

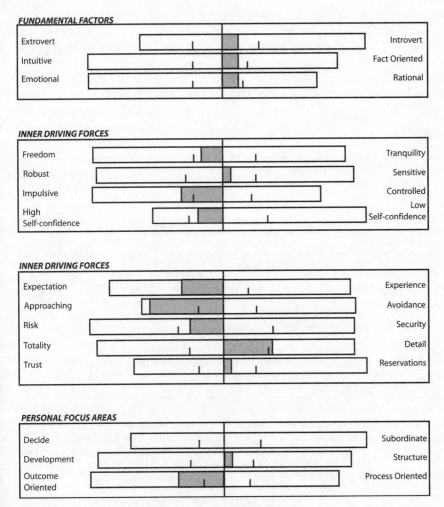

Figure 7-1 Personal Assessment Profile—The Overall Profile

Looking at the profile gives a first impression of a person, but the complete picture requires a thorough analysis of the interrelationships between factors. To perform this interpretation requires extensive training of the person that reads and uses the profile, backed by well-designed expert software. Fully automatic feedback on the Internet? I don't believe in it because people issues and decisions are just too important to leave to software alone.

THE RECRUITMENT PROCESS

A systematic and knowledge-based recruitment process comprises a range of activities, as outlined in Table 7-13.

Table 7-13 Key Steps in a Knowledge-Based Recruitment Process

Step in the recruitment process	Content
Profile job	Analyze job content, goals, obstacles, partners, resources, and relation to overall strategy. Assess current holder of the job (if any) and learn from success or failure.
Profile ideal applicant	Translate job profile into candidate profile—that is, personal factors, personal competencies, education and professional competencies, and experience required.
Announce	Internal/external, printed/web.
Screen applicants	Select a few key criteria and base initial screening on these. Evaluate applicants with unusual backgrounds carefully. Be prepared to deviate from the ideal applicant profile if you have a unique candidate who may bring a completely different resource to the organization that you didn't originally think about.
Profile short-list candidates	Perform a personal assessment profile of all short-listed candidates. Perform personal interview to verify profile and spot strengths and weaknesses not directly reflected in profile.
Select candidate and establish contract	Perform selection as a staged process in which the top candidates meet more employees in several meetings. This gives the applicant an in-depth impression of the organization and more employees can make a contribution to the final selection. In the final negotiation phase, discuss openly fits and misfits between the candidate's profile and the ideal; how strengths can be used to the maximum extent and how misfits should be overcome by both parties.
Fit candidate into organization	Compare profile of new employee with profiles of future close associates and discuss good fits and possible misfits with all involved.
Coach candidate and manager	Focus coaching on potential misfits between associates, in particular, the relationship between the new employee and her manager. Most misfits can be overcome if they are dealt with openly and candidly.
Followup and learning from process	Follow up in general and in particular on identified misfits. Document successes and failures and relate to profiles and misfits.

The process described here is not rocket science, and many companies follow similar procedures including careful profiling of candidates. The main weakness you see repeatedly is that the knowledge gleaned from profiling is not used after the candidate becomes an employee. Nothing systematic is done to make the most out of strengths and to overcome the personality misfits between the new employee and his future colleagues. Such misfits are the rule rather than the exception because the best candidate is not only chosen according to the personal assessment profile, but also because of his unique knowledge, network, or background.

Another weak point seen frequently is followup and learning: Did the misfits that were detected in the selection process actually materialize? Which of the actions that were taken actually helped to overcome the problems? Were there unforeseen problems that arose?

Recruitment is perhaps the HR process where a systematic and knowledge-based approach can generate the most benefit for the resources spent: Excellent people that are coached well to fit into the organization and add something unique to the organization are the key to excellent performance.

Sit back and reflect for a moment. Think of some recent recruitment decisions in your organization that have affected you. Choose the least successful one. Calculate the actual cost of the failed recruitment. Consider if a systematic and knowledge-based recruitment process could have prevented it. What would the return on investment for the systematic recruitment effort have been? Which alternative ways to spend money in your organization yield a higher return?

THE INDIVIDUAL DEVELOPMENT PROCESS

Although most companies have processes in place for individual goal setting, development, and followup, there is often a lack of systematic approach in which this process is linked to the personal assessment profile. Moreover, most processes are designed to meet employer needs rather than to balance employer and employee needs.

The key is to understand both the personal and the professional profile of the person and to take into account both company needs and employee needs and aspirations.

Consider a four-stage process, which should be repeated on an annual basis (see Table 7-14).

Table 7-14 Key Stages of an Individual Development Process

Individual development process	Content
Profile employee	Perform a personal assessment profile of the employee. Perform personal interview to verify profile and to discuss strengths and weaknesses not directly reflected in profile.
Review competencies and goals, prioritize	Review employee education and work experience. Discuss also possible relevant experience from outside work (for example, Scout leader experience). Review personal and professional goals from company and employee viewpoints. Identify gaps and opportunities and prioritize.
Training and on-the-job development	Identify opportunities for on-the-job development through job enlargement, multiple jobs, working with particularly knowledgeable colleagues, or rotation. Identify high-priority formal training needs, if any. Link to personal assessment profile. Identify 3-, 6-, 9-, and 12-month milestones. Execute.
Followup and learning from process	Follow progress through milestone reviews. Analyze in light of personal assessment profile. Learn from successes and failures in process.

In most companies, the opportunities for on-the-job development are given much too low a priority compared to formal training. Often, there is a culture in which employees perceive formal training either a right or a reward. Training budgets are the subject of lengthy discussions, and any reduction in the training budget is seen as a reduction in employee benefits.

I question this approach. Learning and personal development can be stimulated much more effectively by breaking down organizational and physical barriers. Employees can interact freely, and each individual employee can be urged or forced to perform at least one extra job that she is not formally qualified to do. Finding the extra job should be the responsibility and opportunity of the individual. That leads to three interesting changes:

- To everyone's surprise, almost all employees will have spare time (on-the-job) to perform an additional function if the new function is interesting.

- When a person starts doing an additional job, she gets a much broader view of the company than before. There is much less "them" and "us." You will realize that you are one big team where everyone's effort and contribution is essential for success.

- When new eyes begin looking at well-established procedures and habits, it becomes clear that many procedures and habits can be eliminated or improved. Both the employee and the company gain tremendously from fresh eyes addressing old issues.

What happens to the training budget? Simply quit having a budget and make training an opportunity for everyone; however, include the limitation that employees must also contribute some private time if they want to attend a formal training course. The result: On-the-job training takes care of the need for development, from the company's and the employee's points of view. In one case I was involved in, formal training expenses dropped by about 30 percent.

The conclusion is that the personal development process must build on solid knowledge, it must be systematic, and it must balance the needs of both the company and the employee.

 Think of your own experience with formal training, in particular, management training courses. How did it change your behavior? Has it had a long-term effect on your behavior today? Was it worth the investment? How could your job have been redefined to allow you to learn the same things as part of your everyday job?

THE TEAMBUILDING PROCESS

Teambuilding is particularly relevant for project teams that have been established to carry through a project under strong time constraints. Team composition normally reflects the need for different professional qualifications rather than a balanced and healthy diversity of personalities. Therefore, teams and team leaders have a particular need for coaching.

The four-stage process shown in Table 7-15 aims to increase the likelihood that the team becomes successful.

Table 7-15 Key Stages of a Knowledge-Based Teambuilding Process

Teambuilding process	Content
Profile team members	Perform a personal assessment profile of each team member. Perform personal interviews to verify profiles and to discuss strengths and weaknesses not directly reflected in profiles.
Identify strengths, weaknesses, and potential conflicts in team, and prioritize	Cross-tabulate critical personal assessment factors to identify lack of diversity in team, potential conflicts due to opposite profiles on key factors, and other sources of potential problems. Prioritize, modify team if necessary, and coach team leader and individual members as required.
Make team conscious about its composition, strengths, and weaknesses	Discuss cross-tabulations with team. Illustrate consequence of the team's composition by role-playing different situations with different members. Highlight advantage of diversity in team. Turn insight into agreement of division-of-labor between team members. Identify 3-, 6-, 9-, and 12-month milestones. Execute.
Followup and learning from the process	Follow progress through milestone reviews. Analyze in light of personal assessment profiles and team composition. Learn from successes and failures in process.

The key element in this process is to make team members aware of the power of diversity in the team. The process should focus on helping team members understand why the team needs different profiles—that is, some members focusing on the big picture and others focusing on the execution and the details. Teams also need some members that are extrovert communicators and networkers and others who are more introvert—that is, doers.

This sounds easy and logical, but it isn't. Most human beings think that others should be like themselves. If team leaders are extrovert, they seek other extrovert people. If they are risk lovers, they find other risk lovers to work with. But good teams are not like that. They are combinations of people with different profiles. Such diverse teams may not work well together unless you address the issue and do something about it. The purpose of the teambuilding process is to help members understand the need for diversity and thus respect those other members that are different from themselves.

The key to get there is to build on facts—that is, profiles of each individual team member. Intellectually, everyone can understand that if a team consists only of people that love details, there is a high risk that they will never get the big picture. And vice versa: If a team consists only of high-flying visionaries with no one to care about details, chances are slim that they will accomplish their goal. In other words, teams must be diverse, not only along the "totality-detail parameter, but along all relevant parameters, which is about every one of the 15 personal factors in the personal assessment profile.

If you can present facts about the composition of the team, you have a strong means to create that appreciation of diversity. If team members see the cross-tabulations of the distribution of relevant factors in the profile, they understand better their potential role in the team, and they understand the value of having other members that are different from themselves.

If discussing cross-tabulations doesn't prompt this insight, role playing is a good supplement. Define a task—something that benefits from a diversity of knowledge and skills in a team. Compose two teams: One that is rather homogeneous and one that has the required diversity. Let the two teams role play completing the assigned task. Observe the strengths and weaknesses of their different approaches and discuss. You will be surprised.

Use discussions, role plays, and other activities to lead the team into agreeing upon its strengths, weaknesses, and the future division of labor and setting milestones that allow evaluation of the task and how it was completed. Follow up on milestones and learn from the team's successes and failures.

 Have you ever tried to map the profiles of the members of your team in the way I propose? What are the advantages and disadvantages of an overly homogeneous team? For a vastly diverse team?

MANAGEMENT DEVELOPMENT PROCESS

The core of the matter can be reduced to this very simple process if we look upon the development of individual managers (see Table 7-16).

Table 7-16 Key Steps of a Knowledge-Based Management Development Process

Management development process step	Content
Establish a solid foundation	Profile manager, including 360° assessment, and discuss profile in-depth with manager. Recall business objectives and discuss personal goals.
Identify individual milestones	Identify milestones for both business and personal development on a 3- to 12-month basis. Make sure to always include both operational goals and development (change) goals to stress the need for both continuous improvement and change.
Integrate individual and team	Carry through teambuilding process (as discussed earlier) for management team to stress importance of diversity. Share individual and collective milestones and commit. Execute.
Followup and learning	Follow up on milestones, discuss any problems in light of differences in personal profiles and team composition, learn from process, and repeat on an annual basis.

This process is simple. Its core is the fact that managers are different, and there is not one particular personal profile that is ideal for all management work. The challenge is to understand one's own profile and how it affects team members and colleagues. The challenge is also to understand that other people are different and to enjoy the advantages from those differences rather than turning them into destructive conflicts.

Unfortunately, most 360° assessments are rather ritual because they have no connection between the management competencies of the assessment and the underlying factors. In other words, you may be told that you are weak in delegation, but you don't know why. Is it because you are so focused on detail, or is it because you fundamentally don't trust other people? Look for a 360° assessment that links competencies to the personality factors.

 Think for a moment of your own personal experience as a manager. Have you ever been subject to a 360° assessment? What were your strong points and your weak points? Where do they come from?

ORGANIZATIONAL DEVELOPMENT

If you want to implement my recommendations on the collaborative organization, you will recognize that organizational development more or less takes care of itself. The organization is in constant development because you have established the processes that keep the organization moving. There are two things you can do to keep the operation on track:

1. Watch for attempts to build up hierarchies despite the fact that you have abandoned them.

2. Carry through the following simple annual review procedure.

Although a key function for the conventional manager is to keep the organization well organized, the challenge for the person that leads a collaborative organization is to keep it disorganized. Especially in the beginning, former middle managers tend to attempt to establish hierarchies. Such attempts, and the reasons behind them, should be discussed openly. There is always a solution to the underlying problem that does not involve new hierarchies.

The annual review procedure has four main steps, listed in Table 7-17.

Table 7-17 Key Steps in a Knowledge-Based Annual Review Procedure

Organizational development process step	Content
Establish a solid foundation	Profile the organization by assessing where it stands on meaning, partnership, networking, spaghetti organization, and value-based leadership. You may need a more comprehensive survey than the BTC index that I have developed.
Identify strengths and problem areas	The survey must allow you to distinguish between "grass root staff" assessments and opinions of specialists or middle managers because these may differ significantly. Identify the points you need to address most urgently.
Decide upon improvements	Decide upon actions to improve—for example, decision-making speed, communication, cross-functional teamwork, or whatever is most urgent. Set milestones and execute.
Followup and learning	Follow up on milestones. Learn from process and repeat on an annual basis.

This simple process does not address questions about departmental structures, management structures, and the like that normally are key elements in organizational development and change. The reason: There is no more need for such structures if you have established a meaning with what the organization does, if you have made every employee a partner of the company, if you are well networked with external bodies, if you have implemented the collaborative organization, and if you have decided to lead your business through values instead of budgets.

Organizational development then becomes simple. Survey the opinions of the staff, identify weak points, and take actions to change where needed. Follow up to ensure things have changed and repeat the process. It is as simple as that.

 When did your organization last go through a systematic evaluation, and what happened afterwards? Has the process had a lasting effect?

THE INNOVATION POWERHOUSE (IP)

You will be surprised how important the physical design of the workplace is as a tool to shape the culture you want and push behavior in the direction you want. You will be equally surprised how managers believe that a new head office or workplace design itself can change an organization. However, physical change very seldom does the job if the physical change is not combined with organizational and people changes.

Table 7-18 is a collection of things you can do to change ordinary offices into innovation powerhouses, assuming the physical change is not the only thing you do. It is a supporting element in making the spaghetti organization work and sustain.

Table 7-18 Ideas for Creating an Innovation Powerhouse

The innovation powerhouse	Content
Maximize interplay	Productive noise; mobile workplaces; meeting places in the open; meeting rooms without tables and chairs; sofas; beds; coffee bars; and so on.
Challenge conventional thinking	Unconventional furniture, art, 3D design, colors, old and new, classic and modern.
Address all senses	Light, smell, sound, texture. Constant changing environment.
Live the story	Visualize symbols, put the customer in the spotlight, and be unique. Go to the extremes. Tell the story.
Link to the market	Video walls, customer events, and visitors.
Live your values	Make it healthy, be environmentally friendly, no smoking, low sound level, good light, and no dust.

Traditionally, offices were designed to shield the employee from being disturbed by external factors, such as noise from colleagues. This made sense at a time when most work was done individually, such as processing transactions. Such work needed to be precise, and errors could be expensive.

But today, most transaction processing work has been taken over by computers, which means that the work left for humans is primarily less structured work that computers don't do well.

 Before proceeding, think of your own workplace. How would you characterize it?

Less structured work means that the key point is the need to find a nonstandard solution to some nonstandard issue or problem. In other words, more and more work becomes customization and innovation. Such work requires a combination of concentrated thinking and the interaction between staff members with different backgrounds. Therefore, the conventional office or cubicle layout is no longer relevant. There is a need to design workplaces, not for maximum protection, but for maximum interaction between staff.

Ideally, this means that all staff should have the possibility to physically move their workplace from one place in the building to another without barriers as their tasks change. If you sit together with team members that are working on the same project, the noise from them may not be disturbing, but actually productive. I have spent seven years working in such a mobile office environment, and although I sometimes got frustrated over lack of privacy, I quickly realized that the advantages were far greater. The ability to constantly change place as my tasks changed made me understand better what everyone else was doing. I probably lost some short-term efficiency, but I gained tenfold by understanding better the context I was working in. All the little remarks and information picked up informally can never be substituted by formal meetings and written status reports.

Maximum interaction between staff members can also be enhanced through means other than physically changing the workplace. Here, the design of meeting rooms plays a crucial role. I have come to dislike traditional meeting rooms with tables, chairs, a projector, and screens and whiteboards. Such meeting rooms tend to lead to a conservative and defensive behavior by participants. Each participant hides behind a pile of papers or behind a laptop. This leads her to defend her position rather than to be open for dialog. Conventional meetings take time; they are a role play, and often a power play, with little substance.

Imagine taking the table away from such a conventional meeting room. It would change the dynamics of the meeting completely. Participants would be less apt to take defensive positions and more apt to enter into dialog with others.

Plus, the meeting would take less time.

Don't you believe it? It works.

Don't stop there, however. Try to take away the chairs as well. Standup meetings are about 20 percent shorter than similar meetings with chairs and tables. Presentations get a lot shorter. Discussions move quicker to the point. And positions change more rapidly. Plus, the health problems that come from sitting down too much and not moving go away. It is a winner for everyone—except manufacturers of office furniture.

If you think there should be a place for staff to sit down during some meetings, you can substitute chairs with sofas or double beds. Sitting on a circular sofa with no table makes the meeting much more relaxed and prevents participants from automatically defending their traditional places and positions. And a large double bed is a great place for three or four people to sit or lie down while they discuss an issue. It sounds crazy, and it is a little crazy compared to most boring office environments today. It may also look less professional when you want to impress customers by showing them your offices. But, are you sure customers are more impressed by a dull, conventional office environment than a creative and unconventional innovation powerhouse?

What do your meeting rooms look like? Do they stimulate creativity, innovation, and speed? Are they as dull as the rest of the business?

Conventional office buildings often have small kitchenettes for brewing coffee or tea. Move the coffee bars from the kitchenette right into the center of the work area. Make the coffee bar a meeting place. Install whiteboards and workstations to allow for informal standup meetings at the most natural place where different people meet anyway: the coffee bar.

You may say that all this challenges conventional thinking, which is true. But you should go much further in this direction.

Take furniture, for example. After the company has invested millions, tens, or hundreds of millions of dollars in its new head office, it normally looks for new and streamlined office furniture. Grey. Built of steel or aluminum. Possibly with a wooden touch. Everything fits the same streamlined design concept. But are you sure that's the best way to stimulate innovation?

Finland's SOL service company—a cleaning company—abandoned traditional tables. Instead, it used large multiperson organic shaped workplaces that allow changing numbers of employees to work at the same table. This company painted tables in multiple colors and made the entire workplace look like something between Copenhagen's Tivoli Gardens and a kindergarten. It became a fabulously creative working environment.

?What If!, an innovation consultancy company that was awarded the United Kingdom's best place to work 2004, took a different approach. ?What If! let staff members buy used furniture at flea markets or wherever they could find it. It looks strange, but it is highly inspiring, it was cheap, and it gave the staff a unique sense of ownership. Its Fortune 500 clients were impressed to find a firm that dared be different.

Furniture is important, but it need not be conventional to be good. Mix old and modern, new and used. Create surprises and stimulate unconventional thinking.

Look at your organization's furniture and think of the animal that describes the style of it most precisely. Perhaps a donkey? Is the image of that animal what you want your organization to stand for?

This can also happen through variations in light, texture, smell, and sound environment. It is the variation that keeps staff awake and open to change and innovation. Imagine a hard room, a soft room, a cozy room, a professional room, a light and open room, a cage, and many other different rooms for different paths of thinking. Sounds crazy? It is, but you need to be a little crazy to break the curve.

LIVE THE STORY

Think of a company that wants to be perceived as open and friendly. What's the head office like? Steel and glass, armed guards, access control systems, and so on. They don't live their story. And nobody will believe they are open and friendly.

The design and appearance of the company head office and other workplaces is one of the best opportunities to walk the talk. A friendly company must look friendly. A highly professional organization must look professional. A customer-oriented company must put the customer needs in the center.

Here, symbols are a great help. When Oticon made the decision to become (almost) paperless, it not only took away most of the paper. It designed a "paper room" as the only oasis where paper was welcome. Moreover, it put the company shredder in that same room and connected it to the waste container by a wide glass tube that went all the way through the company restaurant. Not hidden, but very visible. Employees and guests enjoyed watching the shredded mail from the morning flow through the restaurant while they were enjoying their lunch. Wow!

Also, Oticon did not only talk about the need for innovation and change. It chose a motto, "Cogitate Incognita" (Think the Unthinkable) and carved it into the large columns at the reception of its head office. It made its values and uniqueness visible and tangible. It told its story through symbols.

Oticon went to the extreme because it needed a fundamental culture change. You can't go halfway from conventional and conservative to innovative if you want to become world leader within your field. You can't expect old habits to go away by just saying they are no longer relevant. You need to constantly remind yourself about what is important.

If you go to the extreme, you gain another advantage: Your company becomes interesting to the media and your customers. Among the blind, the single eyed is king. You can gain millions of dollars in free advertising from being different and interesting to the media. Customers will want to visit your company to see and get inspired from the way you work. Having seen it, they will appreciate your products better. Consumers and dealers will remember the brand name and find it absolutely natural that such an innovative company just has to make great products. Suppliers want to join you as partners. To be a winner, you not only need to have great products. You also must look like a winner.

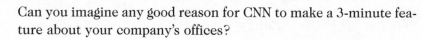 Can you imagine any good reason for CNN to make a 3-minute feature about your company's offices?

LINK TO THE CUSTOMER

Innovation starts with understanding the customer. Not only by surveying the customer base, but by interacting with customers in such a way that you know their needs better than the customers do themselves.

Oticon was pretty far away from customers. Hearing clinics served as intermediaries and earned a high markup to match the extensive customer service that goes with fitting a hearing aid. Oticon was not in retail. But it chose to open a hearing clinic right in the reception room at the head office. Not to go into retail, but to create a constant flow of customers right into the heart of the company. R&D engineers could not avoid seeing real customers sitting in the reception waiting for service on their hearing aids. They were forced to realize that half of the problems with the use of hearing aids were associated with earwax. Until then, probably 1 percent of R&D resources had been allocated to that issue. Also, the average hearing aid user is 72 years of age, but if you are a 32-year old micromechanics development engineer, you most likely design hearing aids that you think are cool. There is no substitute for seeing users every day.

If customers visit your organization, what have you done to make them feel at home and welcome, and to make them walk away with a strong positive impression that will motivate them to buy your product next time?

If you can't bring real customers into your workplace every day, you should arrange customer events and other activities to never forget what a real customer is. With today's technology, you should also consider the possibility to make one wall of the workplace a video wall that shows you 24 hours a day what customers do, how they do it, who they are, and what they look like.

Make it real!

HEALTHY AND SUSTAINABLE

It almost goes without saying that if you want a workplace that supports your vision of an innovative and adaptive organization, you must take every step possible to make the working environment healthy and sustainable:

- No smoking and drinking.
- Clean air, healthy temperature, and little environmental noise.
- Minimum consumption of water and energy, and reuse wherever possible.
- Interaction with the local community—make a positive contribution.

AN INNOVATION POWERHOUSE

Preceding this section is a list of a wide variety of things you can do to make your company an innovation powerhouse. There is one important warning: Don't just copy what other companies have done. Southwest Airlines' head office has thousands of pictures of staff, their homes, and pets—a great idea because that company is obsessed with the idea that they are one big family. But don't let your company imitate one big family if it really isn't one. Be yourself!

CHANGE PROCESS TOOLS (CPT)

It is no simple task to orchestrate change, achieve your goal, and keep your team intact. It takes careful planning of a long process and meticulous attention to detail.

My toolbox has eight tools to help you get there:

- Paint the big picture, but execute step by step.
- Un-learn old habits.
- Plan for early victories.
- Involve skeptics constructively.
- Be open about process, progress, and obstacles.
- Make it real.
- Create momentum.
- Evaluate the process and progress.

There are two fundamentally different approaches to managing change: Either you tell staff members up front what's going to happen, or you make the change little by little to avoid scaring them away. If you choose to implement changes very gently, you most likely need to spend massive amounts of time struggling with middle managers and other employees whose privileges may be threatened. It takes much less effort to go straight to the point. Explain the vision loud and clear, discuss what is in it for everyone, invite contributions (including criticism) and deal with them seriously, modify if necessary, and go! Changes without a clearly spelled out and accepted vision tend to get caught in uncertainty.

After having spelled out the vision, execution comes step by step. If a process takes 12 months, make sure there is a milestone to pass nearly every month. Make the milestone-passing a victory and celebrate it, especially the early victories.

Beware not only of what the organization (including you) has to learn, but also what it has to un-learn. You need an un-learning strategy. One way is to use force, but a more effective approach is to make the new alternative more attractive than the existing situation. For instance, if the change involves moving from small, single-person offices to one, big open office for all—including directors and managers—everyone will be against it. In particular, managers that have enjoyed corner offices with exclusive antique furniture will object fiercely. But try this: Immediately following the move to the new open office, offer the exclusive furniture for sale to employees at an auction in the company storeroom. Everything can be on view from the day you announce the change, so invite employees and managers to take a look at your own, their boss', or their colleague's furniture and imagine how that would look in their living rooms at home. That will change the attitude in one day. Wow, I could buy this furniture cheaply for my home! That's un-learning.

The one factor that determines a project's success more than anything else is employee involvement. If the employees feel ownership of the process and the project, it almost always will be a success. This should be your approach when it comes to change processes. There are few projects that the skeptics think are all stupid. Find one part of the project that they support and involve them in executing that part of the plan. You haven't won them 100 percent, but you have come close.

There are few change processes that don't run into problems and obstacles. Be open about them. Make no secret that there are still unresolved problems, but make it a joint responsibility to tackle them. Don't create a false impression that everything is fine if it isn't. Your staff knows exactly what's on track and what isn't. One way to tackle opposition is to call a two-way meeting, a meeting where you as a manager don't provide initial input, but allow the staff to ask you all the questions they can imagine—including the tough ones.

First, allow for a preparation phase and ensure that there are at least a few prepared questions initially. If you are worried that there will be very few questions, invite participants to work in pairs for 5 to 10 minutes to generate questions. Then, simply have a question-and-answer period. As a variation, you can allow management to ask questions to staff. In closing, you sum up, take actions, and follow up.

If the change you are about to make is a dramatic one, you need to reduce uncertainty. Make a mockup. Make a video or some other simulation that helps staff members understand where they are going. Make it real.

Create momentum—that is, don't allow the change process to stall or slow down. Change may take time, but there needs to be visible progress. If you don't have the resources to progress at the moment, it is better to take a formal pause than to allow the process to slow down.

Last but not least, evaluate the process and follow up. Change processes are the name of the game in the future of any organization, so it is just as important to learn from past change processes as it is to learn from quality problems in production.

Think of the last major change process in your organization that affected you. Was it fun? Did you feel ownership? What would you have done differently to have a much more positive effect?

FOOD FOR THOUGHT

Think of your own organization:

- Take a couple of hours to use the mental model mapper to assess the key elements of your current mental model, where it comes from, whether it is still fully relevant, and what the alternatives could be. Maybe your business model remains sound, but what about your thinking about employees and organization?

- Visit the website www.thesecondcycle.com and perform a self-assessment of your organization. Take a careful look at the 10 second cycle criteria, especially the ones that score low. Why do you think you have scored low?

- Are your organization's values clear enough to allow you to translate them into desired day-to-day behavior for both managers and staff? Have they been implemented and have you created a consensus among all staff about the values and their consequences? Do you dare carry through the consensus building crash process?

- Take a look at your key people management processes (human resource management processes), such as recruitment and individual and team development. Are they truly knowledge based—that is, are they built on solid facts, and do they involve highly refined processes that have demonstrated their efficiency?

- What do your company offices look like? A paper factory? A highly creative working environment? A conservative and conventional company? What sort of person is attracted to working in such an environment? Will that type of person ever make a real world-class breakthrough?

8

Three Live Case Studies

THREE IMPORTANT ORGANIZATIONS IN TROUBLE

This chapter is controversial for at least three reasons:

1. It is about some of the most powerful and important organizations of our time.

2. It argues that these organizations are headed downward on the lifecycle curve.

3. It suggests what these organizations could do and should not do.

How on earth do I believe I have the knowledge, the background, or the position to tell such organizations to fundamentally change their business? Who do you think you are, critics will say?

I don't buy the argument that constructive criticism can and should only come from people in authoritative positions. The organizations I challenge are all vastly important for our societies; they have crucial roles to play and could make an enormous difference in the lives of millions of people. I challenge them in order to make a positive contribution to their future—not the opposite.

I have chosen three very different examples of organizations that I believe have long been caught in the downward cycle:

1. The primary school system
2. The labor unions
3. The U.S. automobile industry

For each case, I argue why. I have limited first-hand experience of them, from discussions with their customers and employees and from the media. I have studied the behavior and communication of their leaders; I have looked into how they phrase their mission, vision, goals, and strategies (to the extent they have any), and I have looked into their origin and history. It is fairly obvious that these organizations are facing problems. Something can be done and must be done to get these organizations back on track.

Do you remember Hans Christian Andersen's fairy tale, "The Emperor's New Clothes"?

It goes like this: The emperor was so fond of clothes that he didn't care about anything else. Two charlatans offered to make him clothes that were invisible to everyone that was "unfit for his position" or simply "impermissibly stupid." Ministers, servants, and the emperor himself all admired the clothes being sown to avoid being seen as unfit for their positions or impermissibly stupid. But one day, while the Emperor paraded through town with his new "clothes," a child said, "He doesn't have anything on!" which was correct.

Consider me to be that child.

METHOD

I have applied the MMM (mental model mapping) tool that you considered in Chapter 7, "The Toolbox."

After having collected information on the case organizations from multiple sources, I have gone through the five-step process:

1. Map the current mental model for the organization.
2. Trace the origin of each aspect of that mental model.

3. Assess whether the situation at origin is still valid.

4. Design a new mental model based on the situation today.

5. Compare and conclude.

I have also offered a few obituaries.

THE CASE ORGANIZATIONS

The three cases have been selected not because they are the worst organizations in the world, but because they represent three very different types of organizations that all need a new start. They illustrate the fact that lifecycles are parallel for all types of organizations, and they show that the same tool can be applied irrespective of sector:

1. A *public institution* that is essential for the future of any society, in particular in the situation where we are moving toward knowledge societies and a knowledge economy.

2. A *not-for-profit* (in principle) movement that has profound influence on the future of millions of people and corporations throughout the world.

3. A group of *large commercial enterprises* in an industry that comprises about 10 percent of gross national product (GNP) in many industrialized countries.

In my view, these organizations share the fate of having once been very successful; however, each faces troubles today.

After mapping their current mental models, I feel confident that their troubles emerge from their own lack of ability to challenge their mindsets and realize that their mental models are outdated. Their mental models are determined by tradition—neither by vision nor by necessity. Plus, each lacks fantasy, energy, or courage to find a new position and carry through the change.

They all seem to have developed blind spots that prevent them from seeing what I consider obvious to outsiders.

To avoid boring you, I have presented the outcome of the MMM in slightly different ways in the three case studies. The MMM process is a creative exercise, and there is no single, correct way to go through it.

THE PRIMARY SCHOOL SYSTEM

SCHOOLS ARE ESSENTIAL FOR THE KNOWLEDGE SOCIETY

In virtually every society, the primary school system is the most important cultural institution. It provides the framework for children and young people's physical, intellectual, and social development; it prepares young people for adult education, work life, and leisure; and it helps young people become familiar with national and world cultures. The primary school system plays a decisive role in motivating young people to take an active role in society. And schools are some of the most important institutions to help children and young people from different ethnic and social groups understand and respect each other. Schools can indeed play an integrating role in multiethnic societies.

Schools provide interesting examples of institutions, once sources of inspiration and progress within their societies. They now have fallen back to a position from which they dramatically need rebirth. Although school systems vary between countries and within countries, there are numerous similarities that justify talking about primary school systems generically. You may find that one or more points are different for the primary school system in your country. You may read this as a general analysis or simply state your country's specific points as you see them.

First, let's take a look at the current mental model as it appears to be for primary school systems that cover the first 10 grades—that is, age ranges between 5 and 16 (see Table 8-1).

Table 8-1 Current Mental Model for Primary Schools

	Current mental model—that is, how most primary schools look upon the world
Students	Students go to school because their parents send them in order that they acquire knowledge and skills. Many students are not motivated to learn. Students are raw materials of the school. They need to be taught a range of subjects in order to pass standardized exams. Students are vastly different due to social, genetic, and other factors.
Teachers	Teachers possess professional knowledge about one or more subjects, which they must transfer to students within the framework of the class. Teachers are responsible for organizing the teaching process within each subject. They choose methods and systems that they think will work best for the class. The teacher's success is measured primarily through student performance in standardized exams.
Parents	Parents send the students to school because they are obliged to do so and because everyone else does so. Parents know that going to school is essential for their children to find a good job and make a living later in life. Most parents support the school, and they want their children to learn as much as possible. Parents are not easy to involve actively in school activities because of other commitments, such as jobs and family activities. Parents expect the school to instill discipline and good manners into the students.
Role of the school (the product)	The school teaches students knowledge and skills within a range of subjects according to the curricula that have been set up by authorities. The school's success is measured by how the students are rated in standardized exams. The primary customer is the school board (most often, the municipality), and the job of the school is to deliver according to standards within budget.
Physical environment	Teaching takes place primarily in classrooms, some of which are equipped for specific subjects such as art, science, or nature studies. Classes take occasional excursions to visit relevant institutions and natural environments. Students spend a limited time of the day at school while most leisure activities and homework takes place outside of the school.
Other educational institutions	The school maintains contact with other educational institutions to achieve a smooth and efficient transfer of students to the school and from the school to other educational institutions. Government regulations specify what students should know while entering and leaving the school.
Technology	The dominating educational method implies that about 25 students gather in one room with one teacher who explains subjects by use of a blackboard with occasional support from audio visuals such as sound, video, computers, and other technologies. Students are asked to solve problems individually and in groups. Technology builds on the classroom as the primary learning space.
Organization	The basic organizational unit is the class of about 25 students. The weekly schedule is divided into one-hour time slots for different subjects. Each subject is taught by one teacher in the class, and subjects are occasionally combined into projects or themes that involve more teachers. The class comprises students of roughly the same age, but within each subject, there are usually great differences between the levels of individual students in a class.

Current mental model—that is, how most primary schools look upon the world	
Organizational learning (continuous improvement)	The school holds regular staff meetings in which teachers are informed about new developments and new rules and regulations. Teachers have an opportunity to suggest improvements to the school. All relevant matters may be brought up for discussion by any staff member. Individual teachers may apply for grants to allow them to attend relevant courses. Funds are, however, very scarce for this purpose.

Of course, this is a rough picture with many variations within each country and between countries. But I believe that the overall picture holds.

This mental model came from an industrial or manufacturing tradition. Think of a factory. Every day at, for example 6, 7, or 8 o'clock, the factory opens its gates and workers enter into the different sections to start work. Work is well defined according to the production plan, and every group of workers has well-defined jobs to do. Every workshop is equipped with relevant tools, and it has a supervisor, who tells workers what to do when. Work follows a precise time schedule with 10- or 15-minute breaks every hour or so. Breaks allow workers to relax, get fresh air, and go to the toilet. Workers start work after the breaks at the same time when the bell rings. The lunch break is longer than other breaks. Workers end their day in the afternoon when the bell rings.

About 100 years ago, schools were designed as teaching factories, and most schools work exactly like that today. Let's look in more detail at the origin of each of the key aspects of the current mental model (see Table 8-2).

Table 8-2 Where the Current Primary School System Mental Model Came From

Current mental model	The current mental model originated from factories as they were 50 years ago...
Students are raw materials that need to be taught in order to pass exams.	This was the dominating thinking of the industrial age. Teaching was the process that transformed children into adolescents that were prepared for further education or training. Parents sent them there for a variety of reasons, but it was seldom the choice of the child to attend school. The end goal was passing the exam with good grades.

Current mental model	The current mental model originated from factories as they were 50 years ago...
Teachers teach specific subjects that they are experts in. Success is measured through exam performance.	The teacher was seen as a specialist to make teaching each subject as efficient as possible. Specialization was also necessary to assure the right professional level. This coincided with Frederick Taylor's thinking on industrial organization. He broke manufacturing work into smaller pieces that could be performed efficiently at good quality. Exams equaled quality inspections of final products from the factory.
Parents send their children to school. They demand performance, but they often don't want to involve themselves.	Whereas children are the raw material, parents are like customers. They want the product at the lowest possible cost and they expect the school to do the job just like they expect all other suppliers to deliver. Parents consider the primary school to be an institution that they pay for directly and through taxes.
Role of the school: An institution that teaches children knowledge and skills. Success to be measured through exam performance.	The school was seen as a factory. It was set up to teach students knowledge and skills. Quality standards were defined though national curricula and quality control was performed through exams. Factory management (the school board) of course required the school to deliver maximum output within budget.
Physical environment for teaching is dominated by classrooms.	The school "factory" required production to be as cost-efficient as possible, which led to the class as the basic organizational unit. Classrooms needed to be efficient to allow students to hear and see the teacher—thus, the conventional classroom design. Classrooms should be isolated from the environment to allow the teaching to take place without interruptions. Moving teaching to other locations (for example, nature) required time and funds for transportation. Conventional industrial thinking minimized the need for transportation and maintained maximum control over the production environment.
Other educational institutions are parallel enterprises that follow similar curricula.	The school needed to ensure portability so that their customers (parents) could safely move from one place to the other without children being left back. Society wanted schools to produce a standard product (graduates) so that downstream educational institutions knew exactly which minimum qualifications their students would have upon arrival. There was little use for cooperation between schools because they basically did the same thing in the same standardized way.
Technology focuses on the classroom—that is, the blackboard and other AV equipment.	The blackboard and, later, other types of AV equipment were the most efficient tools available about 50 to 60 years ago when the current school design emerged. Computers and the Internet were not available. Teacher resources needed to be utilized as efficiently as possible, which led to the combination of the teacher explaining the subject, and the student doing homework.

Current mental model	The current mental model originated from factories as they were 50 years ago...
Organization based on classes, subjects, and 45-minute time slots.	The class is designed as a framework for mass teaching. About 25 students are enough to utilize teacher time efficiently and still a sufficiently small number to allow the teacher to get into dialog with the class and with some individual student in every teaching session. Classes are like batches in a manufacturing operation. The class has also been viewed as a social construction that forces children from different backgrounds to attend school together. The argument has been that forcing children to be part of a class that they do not choose teaches them to work together with all sorts of people.
Organizational learning takes place through formal channels, such as staff meetings.	At the time, 50 to 60 years ago, when the current model for schools became dominant, there was only limited and relatively slow change in performance requirements and the environment of the school. Focus was on cost-efficient delivery (production) according to standards. Organizational learning was not seen as an issue.

The next step is to validate the relevance of the current mental model for public schools by looking at the situation today and tomorrow compared with the origin of the current mental model. There are dramatic changes, in particular, that the whole concept of a teaching factory seems to be outdated.

Today, some people argue that the purpose of primary schools is to teach a certain curriculum to make the students able to pass a standardized exam. However, that view is out of touch with the needs of today's knowledge-based organizations. The purpose of the primary school today is much wider. Of course, all students should learn the necessary skills to function in society. They should also learn to learn and be motivated to learn on an ongoing basis, and they should develop into responsible and autonomous citizens.

That leads in the direction of a very different concept for a primary school:

- Schools are no longer viewed as teaching factories; they need to be world-class *learning environments*. They need to cater for the needs of each individual student. Mass teaching has to be substituted by individual learning.

- *Technology* has improved dramatically with the general availability of personal computers and access to broadband Internet. Software for on-the-spot and remote e-learning is available within almost every subject, thus providing attractive alternatives or supplements to traditional class-based teaching.

- The *knowledge about learning* has increased dramatically during the last two decades. We know much more about the functioning of the brain and the process of learning. We know that different people learn in very different ways, and we know that developing a variety of different intelligences is essential for functioning in work and in life.

- *Children's backgrounds* vary more than before. More countries experience more ethnic variety in local communities, which calls for a more individual approach and different educational methods.

- The importance of *soft competencies*, such as learning, social, and change competencies, has increased along with the increasing speed of change. As innovation occurs primarily through the interplay of a diverse workforce, there is a need for learning much more than individual subjects.

- The industrial (manufacturing) mental model, which was dominant in business in the middle of the twentieth century, is rapidly being substituted with models of knowledge-based and *learning organizations* that are significantly different. The primary school should be the prototype of today's and tomorrow's learning organization.

The conclusion is that the current, conventional, mental model for primary school systems is based on thinking that is largely obsolete. This doesn't mean that all primary schools are failures or that all schools are exactly the way the current mental model has been described earlier. But the big picture is wrong and needs to change.

Therefore, we need to rethink the various aspects of the mental model, which may lead to a radically different—and much more relevant, I believe—type of primary school.

A primary school could become a learning environment instead of today's teaching factory. This idea is developed further in Table 8-3.

Table 8-3 Alternative Mental Model for Primary School System

An alternative mental model for primary schools—that is, how we might look upon primary schools in the future	
Students	Students go to school to acquire knowledge and skills and to develop as human beings. They want to have fun, work with interesting people, do interesting things, and be in charge of their own progress. Students are important resources to enhance the learning process. All students beyond 12 years of age spend 10 to 30 percent of their time assisting other students to learn.
Teachers	Teachers are facilitators that guide individual students through the learning and personal development processes. They have professional knowledge about a range of subjects, which forms part of the learning resources of the school. They coach 10 to 30 students each, perhaps at different age levels. Success is measured by a combination of exams and an assessment of the wider personal and professional development for students.
Parents	Parents are the most important alliance partners to the school. Parents know how important the school is for the future of their kids, and they are keen to be involved in the development of their kids. They know that development of young people is much more than knowledge and skills, and they recognize that they are the primary, responsible persons for the development of their kids—that is, the school is only a supplement to their own efforts.
Role of the school (the product)	The school aims to be the best possible learning environment for every single student. Students work in their individual pace, and the job of the school is to move every student as far as possible along the learning and personal development track. Success is measured in a narrow sense through exams, but the wider and more important perspective is how the school contributes to personal and professional development of the students. The school not only teaches, it offers opportunities to learn and develop.
Physical environment	Teaching takes place in a wide variety of environments inside and outside the school. Nature is taught primarily outdoors; history is taught on location—for example, in museums; and social studies is taught in other relevant locations. Most classrooms have either been combined with others or subdivided into smaller learning cells for individual or small group use. The physical environment is stimulating for all senses, and students spend most of their day at school—also for leisure activities. There is little traditional homework, but many learning activities involve parents and family.
Other educational institutions	Other educational institutions are partners in the learning process of the student. The school takes every effort to get access to all information on the student from other institutions where the student has been before. By knowing the student personally and professionally, the school can customize the learning process for each individual child.

An alternative mental model for primary schools—that is, how we might look upon primary schools in the future	
Technology	The school applies a variety of technologies to support the learning process of each individual student according to need and interest. The teacher inspires the student to combine different learning methods, technologies, and environments to learn faster and to learn about the subject from different angles. To learn a specific subject, the student may take a brief interactive computer introduction to the subject, supplement it by watching a video program, do a small group project, and discuss the outcome with the teacher.
Organization	The basic organizational unit is the individual student. Each student has a tutor or coach that guides the learning process of the student. The coach advises the student on where to focus and how to use available learning resources. The student takes exams according to national requirements, but these are seen as minimum targets only. Teaching at class level is organized only on an ad hoc basis. The coach helps ensure that students work both individually and in teams.
Organizational learning (continuous improvement)	The school is a true learning organization. Staff members constantly interact and involve in each other's work. All staff share good and bad experiences directly and on the school's intranet, which is linked to other schools. Each year, 10 percent of school resources are spent on improvement and development projects with the purpose of improving quality and cost effectiveness. The school requires a payback time of less than three years for all investments and development projects.

The mental model of the primary school described here is radically different from most schools today. Fortunately, in some countries, there are experiments in this direction. The point is that there is much to gain by moving faster toward a new mental model for primary schools.

Table 8-4 summarizes the two mental models.

Table 8-4 Comparing Two Mental Models for the Primary School System

	Current mental model: the teaching factory	Alternative mental model: the learning environment
Students	Students are raw materials that need to be taught in order to pass exams.	Students are essential resources in the learning process. They are in charge of their own learning process.
Teachers	Teachers teach specific subjects that they are experts in. Success is measured through exam performance.	Teachers are resources, facilitators, and coaches. Success is measured by the development of students in a broad perspective.
Parents	Parents send their children to school. They demand performance, but they often don't want to involve themselves.	Parents are essential partners in the learning process. They are highly motivated to involve themselves in various ways.

	Current mental model: the teaching factory	Alternative mental model: the learning environment
Role of the school (the product)	The school is an institution that teaches children knowledge and skills. Success is measured through exam performance.	The school aims to be the best possible learning environment for each child. Success is measured by the development of students in a broad perspective.
Physical environment	Classrooms are the primary physical environments for teaching.	Learning takes place in a wide variety of environments inside and outside the school.
Other educational institutions	Other primary schools are parallel institutions that follow similar curricula.	Other primary schools may follow different paths because the learning process of each child is individual.
Technology	Technology focuses on the classroom—that is, the blackboard and other AV equipment.	Technology focuses on the student. A wide variety of technologies are used as needed, particularly IT.
Organization	Organization based on classes, subjects, and 45-minute time slots.	The organizational unit is the individual student. Learning pace, method, and content is individual.
Organizational learning (continuous improvement)	Organizational learning takes place through formal channels, such as staff meetings.	Schools spend 10 percent of their resources on continuous improvement and innovation of learning methods.

This table illustrates how fundamentally different the two mental models are. Some parents and students may go for the alternative one if given the choice because their mental models are bound to industrial thinking. But if children are to succeed and prosper in the knowledge era, we have to look upon teaching and exams as the means, whereas learning and personal development is the end.

Imagine the perspective if it was possible to convert all public schools into learning environments. The consequences would be dramatic:

- Students would learn more because they are more motivated to learn, they can learn at their own pace, they apply a wider range of technologies, learning takes place at more interesting locations, and they have the opportunity to teach other students and learn from other students. Students would also interact much more intensively with other students of other ages because the same-age classes have been abandoned.

- Students would learn to take more responsibility for their own development and for others. They would develop not only professionally, but also personally. They would learn to learn.

- Parents and other parts of local community would be more involved in the work of the school because learning takes place at a wide variety of locations within the community.

- Students would be better prepared for tomorrow's knowledge-based work that is based on frequently changing teams that represent a variety of different competencies.

- Schools would continuously improve and refine their technology and learning methods.

What are the drawbacks?

Teachers need to dramatically change their roles. They need to spend more hours at the school and work together more with the students. Their day is much less structured, and they need to involve themselves in development work.

Politicians or school boards need to abandon detailed regulation of what happens at what time in the school. The school becomes an organic marketplace with constantly changing processes that are not determined by detailed, scheduled time, but by mechanisms that school boards and politicians cannot control.

It might be more expensive in the short run. There are investments in change of physical premises and the development of technologies—in particular, IT. But in the long run, costs get lower because fewer students drop out of education and fewer students need special education.

Would the conventional primary schools be greatly missed? Look at the obituary that follows:

> The primary school system that has now finally gone dates back more than 200 years. It focused on teaching well-defined curricula to all students. Most students learned to reproduce the knowledge they were required to learn at exams according to the national standard. Teaching took place in highly standardized classrooms, which avoided students being disturbed by irrelevant

factors. The school never fully embraced information technology—in particular, the emergence of the personal computer and the Internet. Students were well suited to continue in the educational system due to standardized requirements and exams. Some students, however, did not fit the mold and never succeeded in the educational system. Their fate is unknown.

In summary, if conventional primary schools did not exist, it would not be difficult to invent something better to replace it. Would conventional primary schools be greatly missed? No!

What if the *overall idea* of a public school was to be as follows?

The Knowledge-Based Primary School

Primary schools are environments designed for learning and personal development. They network with all corners of the local community to provide the widest variety of learning and personal development opportunities for young people. They are fun places to be, they constantly change and improve, and they reward excellent performance by students and staff. They meet national professional and educational standards, but they focus much wider on professional and personal development. They involve every single student and his or her family in the learning process with the aim to maximize the use of each student's resources.

What if such a school suddenly ceased to exist, assuming that the current primary school system remained? The obituary would sound something like this:

The primary school system that has now gone will be greatly missed. The most resourceful students will be referred back to primary schools that focus on the average or below-average student. The less resourceful students will suffer from the lack of individual coaching and attention they have got from primary school until now.

Parents will miss the frequent involvement in the school's life, and society will suffer from the lack of learning and methodological development of the school.

WHY DO PRIMARY SCHOOLS STICK TO THEIR CURRENT MENTAL MODEL—AND WHAT CAN BE DONE?

Primary schools tend to stick to the current mental model for several reasons:

- They feel pressed from all sides and don't feel they have the resources to take charge of their future.
- They don't believe it is possible to carry through radical changes due to rules and regulations, national curricula, and authorities that want to stick to the well-known models.
- They are paralyzed by collective agreements that regulate working hours, working conditions, overtime, and homework. It seems impossible to overcome such agreements, even if the staff of one particular school agreed to do so.
- They perceive that a radical change requires financial and time investments that they would never be allowed to make.
- They lack the fantasy and the courage to think the unthinkable and turn it into reality. They may also think there is only one relevant mental model for the primary school in the twenty-first century.

I think all the preceding obstacles can be overcome if you dare think the unthinkable:

- Start by creating an alliance between teachers, students, parents, and local politicians that are willing to break the rules to get a better school.
- Drop all rules and regulations that prevent you from creating tomorrow's learning environment.
- Design tomorrow's school with complete disrespect for conventional thinking, rules, and regulations.
- Show the great advantages of a new and different approach to learning to students, parents, teachers, and local community.

- Make a list of all the limitations that prevent you from implementing the vision and confront every authority with the part of the limitations that they are responsible for. Demand a change—at least for a test period—and make no secret that you will disclose all examples of authorities that do not cooperate.

- To start the change, you need money. Make sufficient short-term savings (for example, substitute one vacant teacher position with older students teaching younger colleagues, or make students do the cleaning of the school under adult supervision) to allow you to make the first investments in change.

- Proceed gradually and use the change process tools found in Chapter 7.

It can be done!

 What do you think? Would you send your children into a teaching factory or into a learning environment?

THE LABOR UNIONS

LABOR UNIONS ARE IMPORTANT PLAYERS IN THE KNOWLEDGE SOCIETY

I have chosen labor unions as a case study because these organizations play a major role in society even though the basis for their establishment has changed dramatically.

Labor unions are powerhouses. They base their power on the fact that they represent and control hundreds of thousands or millions of workers that have delegated their freedom to negotiate financial and other working conditions with their employers to the labor union. The power of labor unions also rests with the fact that they have entered into agreements with employers that oblige employers to comply with certain rules and standards and to negotiate any change thereof with the labor unions involved.

This means that labor unions legally can put an employer under severe pressure, which in the end can put the company out of business if the conflict is not resolved. Employees that do not follow the rules can be excluded from the union, which may lead to difficulties finding a job and making a living.

The fact that labor unions represent significant shares of the population creates a power base toward governments. Unions do not control how their members vote, but they can make life difficult for any government if they mobilize their members against the government as such or some specific policy item.

Unions are often seen as almost charitable organizations. They enjoy tax privileges in many countries due to tax deductibility of membership fees and other items.

However, unions are far from charitable organizations. They are set up to represent the interests of specific groups of the population toward employers and the government. Nonmembers are not represented.

In the following analysis, you find a review of the current mental model of labor unions. There are significant differences between the function of unions in different parts of the world. In this context, we focus on labor unions in the western industrialized world—that is, Europe and the U.S. Even within these regions, there are significant differences between labor unions. The analysis is therefore limited to items that are largely generic.

First, let's take a look at the current mental model of labor unions shown in Table 8-5.

Table 8-5 Step 1: The Current Mental Model of Labor Unions

Key aspect	Current mental model
Members	Members are workers in danger of being exploited by employers. They must stand united against employers to effectively fight for their rights.
Employers	Employers are capitalists that look upon workers purely as production factors. Employers will use any means to maximize profit. They will hire and fire employees according to short-term need, and they will strive to pay minimum amounts per working hour.
Role of the labor union (the product)	The union protects members against exploitation by their employers. They bargain collectively for members, and their success is measured on their ability to constantly improve wages and working conditions for members. Bargaining is fundamentally a zero-sum game.
Other unions	Ideally, all staff should belong to one single union to gain maximum strength in the fight against the employer. Different labor unions tend to tolerate each other best if members have significantly different educational backgrounds or vocations.

Key aspect	Current mental model
Non-unionized employees	Nonmembers are enemies because they are free riders that benefit from the efforts of the unions without paying the bill. They weaken the power of the union.
Nonmembers	Unions exist for the benefit of their members only. Nonmembers are irrelevant, and the union's social responsibility is limited to helping members improve their working conditions.
The individual member	The individual member is an instrument for the collective good. It is more important to improve working conditions and wages for members in general than it is to cater to individual needs.

This mental model emerged from an industrial or manufacturing tradition in which unions fought for the rights of their members against employers that had no sense of responsibility toward workers. It was probably reasonably well justified 50 or 100 years ago. At that time, labor unions played a much-needed role to ensure that workers were given reasonable conditions and fair pay. The game was a true zero-sum game—that is, if one party gained something, the other party lost the same amount.

Let's look a little more in detail into the origin of each of the key aspects of the current mental model (Step 2 of the MMM), whether the situation has changed (Step 3 of the MMM), and how this ought to inspire unions to define a new mental model for their work (Step 4 of the MMM). In this case, we will go through Steps 2, 3, and 4 of the MMM process for each aspect (see Table 8-6).

Table 8-6 Mental Model for Labor Unions and Their Members

Key aspect	Current mental model	Origin	Relevant today?	Possible new mental model
Members	Members are workers in danger of being exploited by employers. They must stand united against employers to effectively fight for their rights.	Industrial unrest in Europe in the nineteenth century. Employers viewed the workforce as a production factor only. Workers could easily be substituted by others.	No. Motivated and loyal employees are essential for value creation. They cannot easily be substituted.	Members want to make an active contribution to wealth creation in society together with employers. They expect to receive a fair share of the wealth they help create.

The striking point is that labor unions in general still treat members as weak, uninformed workers that first of all need protection against evil employers. However, many businesses have long ago abandoned this thinking because they have realized that such relationship between staff and management will never make it possible to become world-class.

Moving on to the mental model of labor unions against employers, we see a similar picture (see Table 8-7).

Table 8-7 Mental Model for Labor Unions and Employers

Key aspect	Current mental model	Origin	Relevant today?	Possible new mental model
Employers	Employers are capitalists that look upon workers purely as production factors. Employers use any means to maximize return. They hire and fire employees according to short-term need, and they pay only minimum amounts per working hour.	The labor market 100 to 150 years ago.	No. Some employers still view staff as a production factor only, but the trend toward partnership is very strong.	Employers strive to maximize wealth creation in the firm together with employees. They are prepared to share the wealth created with employees so that employees are satisfied with the deal—that is, they want to stay with the company—and they strive to continuously improve the business.

This opens an opportunity for the labor union to play a new and much more dynamic and relevant role, which is fundamentally different from today's mental model (see Table 8-8).

Table 8-8 Mental Model for the Role of Labor Unions

Key aspect	Current mental model	Origin	Relevant today?	Possible new mental model
Role of the labor union (the product)	The union protects members against exploitation by employers. They bargain collectively for members, and their success is measured by constantly improving wages and working conditions for members. Bargaining is a zero-sum game.	The labor market 100 to 150 years ago.	No. Most members don't view the employer as an enemy. They know that their job only exists if it is competitive in a global context.	Unions are instruments to maximize wealth creation in all types of organizations. They help develop organizations that are competitive, innovative, flexible, and efficient. They help ensure that employees get a fair share of the wealth created.

Based on this analysis, I suggest that labor unions redefine their role to become partners of both members and corporations to maximize competitiveness and wealth creation. For employees in western Europe and the U.S. (and other industrialized countries), the employer is not the enemy. The enemy is the risk of losing competitiveness, either through outsourcing of employee jobs to low-cost countries or through the company's loss of competitive power and thus market share. In general, employees in the western world do not want higher wages or shorter working hours if that forces the employer to move their jobs to China.

The key challenge for employees is to remain competitive so that they can keep an interesting and secure job that will offer them opportunities to grow and develop. The union can choose to play a major role in this process. It has the advantage of being able to gain both the employee's and the employer's confidence. It can build up world-class expertise in competency management and human resource management in general. It has contact to other employers inside and outside the industry, and it knows the individual employee's background and wishes.

This could also change the relationship between unions (see Table 8-9).

Table 8-9 Mental Model for the Labor Union and Other Unions

Key aspect	Current mental model	Origin	Relevant today?	Possible new mental model
Other unions	Ideally, all staff should belong to one single union to gain maximum strength in the fight against the employer. Different labor unions tend to tolerate each other best if members have significantly different educational backgrounds or vocations.	The labor market 100 years ago.	No. One union is no longer important to gain influence. Different unions for employees with different functions could inspire unions to focus in particular on their member's common challenges and opportunities to contribute to wealth creation. In a partnership model, more than one union does not create a problem.	Other unions are partners. Different people may be served best by different unions as long as unions work together toward a goal. One size may not fit all, and a variety of unions with different approaches may be the best solution for some companies.

The key point is whether unions see themselves as opposites or partners to employers. In the partnership model, unions appreciate input from other parties, including unions that cover categories of employees other than their own membership. Unions need to realize that the overall goal of value creation in the company can best be achieved by different parties working together.

The attitude toward non-unionized employees and nonmembers also must change (see Table 8-10).

Table 8-10 Mental Model for Labor Unions and Non-Unionized Members and Nonmembers

Key aspect	Current mental model	Origin	Relevant today?	Possible new mental model
Non-unionized employees	Nonmembers are enemies because they are free riders that benefit from the efforts of the unions without paying the bill. They weaken the power of the union.	In a fighting situation, the union's position is seriously weakened by employees that are not members.	No. The rationale for fighting is passing away for more and more businesses.	Non-unionized employees are viewed as customers that have not yet bought the product. They are tempted to join through sales and marketing efforts.

Key aspect	Current mental model	Origin	Relevant today?	Possible new mental model
Nonmembers	Unions exist for the benefit of their members only. Nonmembers are irrelevant, and the union's social responsibility is limited to helping members improve their working conditions.	Originally, labor unions were financially weak. They needed every dollar they could get.	Partly. Labor unions are wealthy in many countries, but obviously want to avoid free riding. However, new members are attracted by offers they can't resist—not by force.	Nonmembers are viewed as customers that have not yet bought the product. They are tempted to join through sales and marketing efforts. The social responsibility of the union extends to all parts of society, including nonmembers.

Non-unionized employees and nonmembers will have to be seen not as free riders, but as potential customers (members). In today's environment in the western world, there are very few people who really need union membership. While employers and unions move toward a partnership model, it will be increasingly difficult to use union power to force members to join. Unions need to offer a package to potential members that they cannot resist.

Unions have to reconsider their offerings to members (see Table 8-11).

Table 8-11 Mental Model for the Labor Unions and the Individual Member

Key aspect	Current mental model	Origin today?	Relevant mental model	Possible new
Individual member	The individual member is an instrument for the collective good. It is more important to improve working conditions and pay for members in general than it is to cater to individual needs.	The labor market situation 100 years ago.	Individual members do not accept to be viewed primarily as instruments for the collective good. They become members because they feel they can benefit personally.	The individual member is a customer and a colleague. The union must constantly add value to the individual, and the advantages of joining should be obvious—also for the highest qualified employees. The service package is customized.

Although membership used to be fully standardized, today's and tomorrow's members require a flexible solution allowing them to customize their membership package.

In summary, tomorrow's mental model for labor unions is a partnership for value creation.

The mental model of a labor union that I describe is radically different from the situation in most countries today.

However, there is much to gain for labor unions, individual employees, and society by moving faster. Look at the overall idea of today's or (hopefully) yesterday's labor union. Its *reasons to exist* were:

The Current Labor Union

Labor unions are organizations of employees that have been set up to negotiate and fight for employee rights against employers. Successful labor unions help members achieve maximum financial benefits and working conditions including job security.

Try to perform the obituary test to the labor unions that followed this mental model:

The labor unions that have now gone were established more than 100 years ago in a period of labor unrest particularly in Europe and the U.S. They managed to deliver vastly improved financial and working conditions during most of the twentieth century, and they achieved a strong bargaining position against employers. In the first decade of the twenty-first century, labor unions failed to adjust to the fundamentally changed relationship between employers and employees and continued their fight for still higher wages, shorter working hours, and improved working conditions. This fact made many members lose interest, which led to a rapid deterioration of labor unions that has now resulted in bankruptcies and dissolutions of many formerly strong unions throughout the western world.

What if *the overall idea* of labor unions were to be as follows?

The Future Labor Union

Labor unions serve as partners with employers with the overall purpose of maximizing value creation in the firm. Through this process, labor unions add to firms' competitive position, which creates and preserves jobs. Labor unions enter into partnership agreements that ensure a fair balance of risk and financial gains between employers and employees. Labor unions have acquired world-class competencies in human resources management (HRM) to match similar competencies of employers. Unions have achieved today's strong position because they have managed to achieve the confidence of both employers and employees while offering unique insight and counseling to both employers and employees.

If this type of labor union went out of business, its obituary would be as follows:

The labor unions that have now gone were created as a consequence of the changing roles of employees in knowledge-based enterprises. They caught on quickly because the decline of conventional labor unions had left a vacuum for both employers and employees. Contrary to expectation, the changed role of labor unions prompted an increase of membership. Employees chose membership not because they were forced to by collective agreements, but because the work of the labor union and its partnership with employers created substantial value for the individual employee. Employees will miss this value creation, and they will be left with the challenge of managing their value on the labor market alone.

WHY DOESN'T IT HAPPEN—AND WHAT CAN BE DONE?

Labor unions are conservative. They enjoy a comfortable power position, and they share this position with employer's associations. Both parties on the labor market employ significant numbers of people, including a number of attractive and well-paid management positions. Labor unions and employer's associations have little motivation to rock the boat. Why fix it if it ain't broke?

The problem is that is will be broken shortly. Employees will increasingly leave unions, and employers will find it less interesting to negotiate with unions that reside in mental models that are clearly obsolete.

The majority of players on the labor market will reject my analysis. But some employers and labor unions will start to realize which way the wind blows. I hope they will show the courage of challenging their long-serving mental models and adopt new ones that reflect today's reality.

 Reflect for a moment about your perception of a labor union. Do you think the current mental model for labor unions is a fair description of reality? Is it relevant today? Could you imagine what would happen if labor unions changed their mental model? Could you imagine them taking a new role in society? Why didn't this happen long ago?

THE U.S. AUTOMOBILE INDUSTRY

THE INDUSTRY OF INDUSTRIES

When I visited www.gm.com in June 2005 to check some financial data, I was met by the flashing message: "For the first time in history, everyone in America gets the GM employee discount." That took away my last doubt whether it was relevant to present the U.S. automobile industry in general, and General Motors in particular, as a case story in this book illustrating how companies miss the boat by applying mental models that are long outdated.

The U.S. auto industry—namely, the Big Three (General Motors, Ford, and Daimler-Chrysler)—employs more than half a million people, and its revenues amounted to just under $500 billion (U.S. dollars) in 2004. It was once called "the industry of industries" due to its leading role in shaping the model of the large multinational corporation of the twentieth century. Ford invented large-scale mass-production, and Alfred P. Sloan of GM created the management structure that is still dominant in large corporations throughout the world.

The U.S. auto industry was, for decades, the case story studied by students and managers that wanted to understand the essence of the industrial corporation.

Not any more.

GM and Ford bonds have been downgraded to just above junk status. Growth and profit forecasts have been abandoned, and market capitalizations have fallen below several Danish companies that used to be dwarfs compared to GM and Ford. GM—about 300 times the size of Oticon in revenues and equity—enjoys a market capitalization that is only seven times higher than Oticon's.

This has inspired me to analyze the mental models that seem to dominate GM and Ford management (Chrysler is a different case, now being part of the German Daimler-Chrysler Group) and to bluntly challenge them.

GM's 321,000 employees manufacture about nine million cars per year from factories in 32 countries (2004). The website boasts that the company, for the fourth consecutive year, set industry sales records in the U.S., its largest market, for total trucks, pickup trucks, and sport utility vehicles. The website does not display the company's significant loss of market share for light vehicles in the U.S. that has now dropped below 25 percent in the first quarter of 2005. During the booming 1990s, GM returned an average of 3 percent on capital. Since 2000, the figure has been even lower.

Not all auto manufacturers have experienced a similar development—in particular, Toyota. The Japanese company is now challenging GM as the world industry leader, consistently growing faster and more profitably.

Something is rotten in the city of Detroit. But why?

Take a look at the mental model summary for General Motors, in particular, and the U.S. auto industry, in general, in Table 8-12. In this example, I show the entire analysis in one table.

Table 8-12 Aspects of GM's Mental Model

Aspect	Current mental model	Origin	Validation	Possible alternative
Customer	Customer is king—that is, customer surveys determine product strategy.	Alfred Sloan, as a reaction to Ford's manufacturing focus.	Still relevant, but insufficient in times of rapid innovation in the marketplace.	Anticipate customer needs; get in front of customer; shape the future.
Product	What customers currently express that they want. Mainstream rather than niche focus.	Dates from times with slow changes in demand and only little innovation from competitors.	Gradually irrelevant as competitors innovate more and consumer demand becomes more fragmented.	Cutting edge products for mainstream customers. Mass customization. Shape the future industry.
Environment	Fuel efficiency only minor issue short term. Long-term solution is hydrogen-powered cars.	Until recently, energy and CO_2 issues have not been high on the U.S. consumer agenda.	Energy and CO_2 issues rapidly moving higher on the agenda.	Make environmental consciousness the hallmark of the business.
Workers	Workers are production factors. Unions are opposites that must be tolerated.	1920s when workers performed routine operations that could easily be made by others.	No longer relevant. Workers are highly skilled and must participate in ongoing improvements.	Make the workforce the key asset of the business. Make them partners and associates instead of a liability.
Management	Financial or "professional" background as opposed to "car people."	Reaction to the industry's financial problems in the 1990s, when finance people were brought in to rationalize and downsize.	Has made the company lose its "love for cars"—that is, its leadership. Has prompted a "reduction" and "saving" culture contrary to an innovative culture.	Revolution needed to refocus company on shaping the industry. Value-based leadership, spaghetti organiza-tion, and partner-ship. We love cars.

Aspect	Current mental model	Origin	Validation	Possible alternative
Marketing	Mainstream marketing to mainstream customers. Response to 9/11 has been massive discount programs that have taken away profits.	Once enjoyed more than 60 percent share of the U.S. market; GM defined and lived from the mainstream market.	Mainstream markets shrink in all product categories. Customers are looking for solutions that match their specific needs.	Introduce new brands aimed at specific customer groups, such as young people. Sharpen brand values to reflect revolution. Take lead on the Internet.

General Motors' claim to fame was its marketing strategy that offered consumers more choice, more models, more colors, and more brands. Although Ford refined its assembly line manufacturing in the 1920s, GM went out of its way to give customers what they wanted. This seems to be the origin of GM's current mainstream product and marketing strategy. The customer is king; this is demonstrated in GM's and Ford's new U.S. models, which appear to be based strictly upon customer demands gleaned from focus groups and other types of customer surveys.

This strategy was successful at a time when demands were relatively stable, and there was not much innovation from (overseas) competitors. For decades, Detroit's cars reflected the conventional American taste for heavy boxes of iron with silent engines, impressive design, and comfort in the form of smooth riding. Marketing focused on large mainstream segments.

In this environment, European and Japanese manufacturers had a relatively easy time filling niches for sports cars, other premium priced and luxury cars, plus small economical cars. GM and Ford continued to refine their mental model of mainstream cars that were heavy, large, smooth, powerful, and fuel inefficient. Their attempts to meet the overseas competition were only half hearted. Instead of challenging their own mental model, the U.S. automakers used their financial muscle to acquire European luxury and sports car manufacturers such as SAAB, Volvo, and Jaguar without ever fully benefiting from the acquisitions.

Being a relatively small segment, the lack of success in the premium price market never had a major influence on the U.S. automakers. They continued to do business as usual.

The small car market was a much more severe issue. Japanese manufacturers—in particular, Toyota—slowly but surely carved out niches of this much larger segment during the 1980s and later. Detroit responded by introducing stripped-down and smaller versions of mainstream U.S. cars that were at best "me, too" products. Never did the U.S. industry challenge its dominating mental model of a car. It just offered more of the same as usual, in slightly smaller versions.

U.S. consumers then discovered that not only did Japanese cars offer better performance—in particular, more miles per gallon—but they were also more reliable and were backed by a better dealer network. The U.S. auto industry responded by a drive for quality, which gradually brought it on par with the Japanese. No leadership, only improvement of the current mental model.

Why did two of the world's formerly most successful and largest companies not respond proactively, although the need seemed obvious for more than a decade?

Nobody seems to have an authoritative answer, but both companies seem to have been caught in the cycle as described in Chapter 2, "The Second Cycle: A New Paradigm." They became larger and older and were successful for many years. They held high positions on the Fortune 500 and other similar lists of the largest companies, and their managers were featured as some of the most powerful persons in corporate America. They developed many of the symptoms of the virus of success, and they were blinded by their self-perception of greatness, just like any other company that is caught in the cycle. Size doesn't make things easier; it only makes it more difficult to recognize the reality of the situation and to challenge one's mental model. The larger you are, the more you have to lose.

GM's financial troubles have been associated with the high social costs of health programs and defined benefit pension schemes of their workers. These schemes date back decades, but were significantly improved (from the worker's point of view) in 1999 when Ford, GM, and Chrysler managements accepted very generous terms on the background of booming sales and profits from sales of SUVs and light trucks. The following downsizing of GM's manufacturing operations in the U.S. has made this burden relatively greater. Today, GM has about 2½ pensioners per worker in the U.S. Social costs amount to about $2,000 per vehicle manufactured in the U.S. (2004), and there seems to be little hope of a new deal with the United Auto Worker's Union (UAW) in the current climate.

I believe the time for radically changing the mental models of the two dominant U.S. automakers is long overdue. The analysis leads to seven key points (related to GM):

1. GM must find a new meaning for the company. Perhaps it should go for the position to provide vehicles for sustainable, fast, comfortable, safe, and fun transportation instead of just "more great new cars and trucks."

2. GM must become proactive in its product and marketing strategy, developing cutting-edge products that can reposition GM as a leader—not a follower in niche and mainstream segments.

3. GM must take the lead in fuel-efficient, yet high-performance vehicles today—not in 2020, when hydrogen-powered cars are due to take off in large volumes.

4. GM must turn its marketing strategy to sell value to customers instead of discounts. GM cannot realistically achieve cost leadership in the foreseeable future.

5. GM must change its company and management culture radically to become less conservative, more innovative, more flexible, more courageous, and more diverse. More meaning, more values, more leadership, and more spaghetti!

6. GM must establish a partnership with all employees with the aim to not only survive, but to take GM back into the league of world-leading corporations. The future GM (if any) is a knowledge based rather than an industrial corporation.

7. GM must develop its relationships with both suppliers and distributors to become strategic partnerships instead of buy-sell relationships.

The seven points reflect the criteria for future-oriented companies in Chapter 3, "Meaning." They constitute a radically different mental model from today's model.

Perhaps it is too late.

In that case, I should like to offer an obituary for GM:

> General Motors Corporation was founded in 1908 and grew to become the world's leading and largest industrial corporation under the leadership of Alfred P. Sloan. Mr. Sloan pioneered principles of marketing and company organization that have had and still have a profound influence on management thinking and practice throughout the industrialized world. At its peak, GM supplied about 60 percent of all cars to the U.S. market. Between 2000 and 2005, GM manufactured and sold about 10 million cars per year.

The company lost market share primarily to Japanese and European competitors due to conventional thinking in all aspects of the business—in particular, because of lack of innovation in product development and marketing. Top management responded by downsizing, but continued to apply the mental models of the past. GM never moved out of the industrial mindset and therefore missed the opportunity to become a knowledge-based business. In the last 15 to 20 years, management was dominated by people with a professional and financial background who lacked the feel for the business where the rubber meets the road.

I obviously hope that this obituary will never have to be written. I trust GM and Ford still have time to act, and I believe the U.S. and the world needs car companies that will take the lead in providing transportation that is more sustainable, faster, more comfortable, safer, and more fun.

WHY DIDN'T IT HAPPEN LONG AGO?

Automakers, like many other large corporations, tend to stick to their current mental models:

- They feel under pressure to meet short-term goals from financial markets, although this short-term focus may destroy value long term.

- They are managed by people with a financially oriented mindset. If your brain thinks only in profits and losses (P&L) and assets and liabilities, your corporate fantasy will most likely be limited to downsizing, outsourcing, mergers, and acquisitions.

- They are paralyzed by decades of conflicts with the UAW, and they can't think the unthinkable—that the former enemy could become a partner.

- Their top management was brought up in the industrial age, and it cannot imagine that a radically different mental model is necessary to become successful in the knowledge economy.

I think all the preceding obstacles can be overcome if automakers dare make the unthinkable a reality: search for a new meaning, create consensus among major stakeholders, change relationships into partnerships, create a new culture, and show leadership.

It can be done.

 What do you think about my analysis? Is it relevant? Will the U.S. automakers ever realize that the world has changed since their golden age? What would you do if you were CEO of General Motors?

CONCLUSION

These three examples of organizations have much in common:

- They are large; however, two of them are comprised of many smaller entities (local schools and local labor union units).

- They can be found almost all over the world.

- They are vastly important for our lives today and in the future.

- They were established by people with visions: the primary schools were to educate the population and eradicate illiteracy, the labor unions were to empower workers and ensure them a fair share of the value they created, and the U.S. automobile industry wanted to get America rolling—that is, to make Americans mobile.

- Their original visions have been fulfilled to a high degree: very few people in the industrialized world are without basic reading and other skills, workers have good conditions and are well paid, and the U.S. is rolling like no other country in the world.

- Their successes have not made them establish a new and radically different vision: Primary schools continue to do in principle the same job they have done since the beginning, labor unions basically do more of the same, and the automobile industry sticks to its knitting, perhaps adding financial services and other ancillary activities to their empires.

- They are all in a crisis that positions them at a late stage on the lifecycle curve (the first cycle): primary schools are rightly criticized for not delivering, labor unions sometimes are destructive, and the U.S. auto industry is in commercial and financial trouble.

- None of them seem to realize the seriousness of their situation to the extent that they seriously question their mental model and define a new platform for a possible second cycle. They are well into the death cycle, and few people believe they will ever get out of it.

In analyzing how these three organizations could actually break the cycle, it is clear that the difficult part is convincing their respective leaderships to step back and look at the mental models that have built up over decades or centuries. The real problem is the diagnosis and how to address that diagnosis. The apparently insurmountable obstacle is to realize that their history and traditional way of working has become outdated and irrelevant.

There may be two explanations: The leaders are really blinded, or they know there is a problem but are not willing to, or are not motivated to, deal with it. After all, they may only have three or five years left before retiring, so why not leave the dirty work to the next generation?

My advice is not to leave the dirty work to the next generation, but to make the transformation an exciting journey into the future. All three organizations have a wealth of relevant knowledge and the people who can put that knowledge to work. All organizations still have goodwill and a strong position in their respective markets. All organizations can find lots of important problems to tackle or opportunities to address:

- Primary schools need to prepare coming generations for quality of life, responsible life, and productive life in a radically different knowledge society.

- Labor unions are faced with an enormous responsibility and opportunity in helping workers in industrial countries succeed in the knowledge society with much deeper global division of labor.

- The U.S. automobile industry has the greatest opportunity ever: to create transportation that is environmentally sustainable, yet safe, fast, reliable, comfortable—and fun!

Can you wish for more?

FOOD FOR THOUGHT

Choose an organization that you know. Use the mental model mapper tool to perform an analysis of its current mental model, how it originated, whether it is still relevant, and possible alternatives. Do you think its management team has ever made an assessment like this?

Think of the primary school system in your country or region:

- Does the mental model in the book reflect the organization's situation?

- How would a real, world-class school look like?

- How do you think you could persuade someone to offer her school for an experiment: "The public school of the twentieth century."

Think of your local labor unions:

- What is their mental model, where did it come from, and how should it be changed?

- How would you organize a labor union today?

- Do the labor unions have a future at all?

Take a look at the U.S. auto manufacturers:

- Judging from their products, what do you think their mental model is?

- What do you think they could have done or should do to address the issue of high labor costs in the U.S.—in particular, health- and pension-related costs?

- Why are Japanese manufacturers—in particular, Toyota—more successful than their U.S. competitors?

Look at the three case studies. What do they have in common? What could be their new reason for being?

9

Conclusion

By this point, you realize that many mature organizations need reinvention. If you are helping your company reinvent itself as needed, you need to go beyond merely being flexible and responsive. Reinventing a mature company often means changing its mental model, including its approach to customers, suppliers, employees, and everyday working habits. It means constant evaluation and awareness of the big picture, as well as awareness of the details of getting everyday business accomplished using the tools shared in this book or developing your own. It means being ahead of change instead of being behind it.

There is a great untapped potential in revitalizing mature organizations within the private and public sectors and within civil society. If tapped, mature organizations could become more relevant and valuable to their customers, they could enjoy greater growth and profitability, and they could create more and better jobs for their staff.

The potential remains untapped for two reasons:

1. Mature organizations tend to think that they already make the most out of their potential; that is, they believe they are doing the right things. They behave like they are deaf when their fundamental beliefs are questioned. The more successful they are or have been, the worse their hearing becomes.

2. If mature organizations somehow realize that they have a problem (or an opportunity) to improve, they lack the tools to carry through the necessary change, particularly because the transformation that they need is different from what they know. Mature organizations are highly experienced in improving the way they do things, but they lack the capability to question whether they do the right things at all.

You may well be the part of the problem: Are you so much a part of your organization's success that you have lost the ability to step back and look upon your organization at a distance? Managers in particular need to constantly remind themselves that their mental model must never become one of tradition; it should be one of necessity, oriented toward the future instead of the past.

Three factors make mature organizations easy targets for the virus that turns success into failure. The three factors are *size, age,* and *success.* While organizations grow, they get more management layers, they establish more departments, and they introduce more and more rigid procedures. As they mature, they establish routines and traditions that tend to make business as usual the norm rather than the exception. Although they enjoy success, they become complacent, lazy, and even arrogant, eventually forgetting the needs of their customers that were the initial source of their wealth and success.

One surprising observation is that mature organizations normally don't realize the progression of their transformation from success to failure. They watch their core business become cash cow business; that is, a stagnating business that generates income and cash, and they apply their surplus cash to acquire other businesses that they may consolidate into the existing business. The acquisitions add to the short-term top line and improve short-term bottom line through downsizing and rationalization. If there are no such acquisition opportunities available, mature companies pay out larger dividends or buy back shares from the market.

Mature organizations also become increasingly blinded by their current mental models:

- They fail to discover changing customer needs.
- They are bound by marketing and sales channels that gradually become obsolete.
- They stick to product concepts because they fit existing business models.
- They treat employees the same way their managers were treated in their early years.
- They use their bargaining power to put unfair pressure on suppliers and intermediaries.
- They increasingly focus on management bonuses and other incentive programs.
- They believe in short-term financial performance and shareholder value creation as the only genuine criteria for success.

For many organizations, this process has happened in parallel with the overall change from the industrial era to the knowledge-based society, and many of their shortcomings have become more serious because of this change in society.

The second cycle platform is a new social construction, a new framework for doing business in the knowledge economy. If it is widely accepted, mature organizations (public and private) can jump out of the conventional lifecycle into sustained second cycle growth. This will benefit shareholders through much greater value creation. It will benefit customers through more innovative and customized products. Employees will benefit from better jobs and a fair share of the value they create. Suppliers will enjoy win-win partnerships with their customers, and society will benefit from organizations that serve a meaning beyond profitability. This could fundamentally change not only the business community, but the world.

In general, the move from first cycle to second cycle organizations will happen slowly and gradually, as did the change from agriculture toward the industrial society 150 years ago. Those countries that industrialized faster gained competitive advantage and wealth over those that moved slowly. The same will happen for those companies or countries that manage to transform current social constructions (hierarchical, functional, and bureaucratic organizations) to the realities of the knowledge economy. Your choice is whether you want to lead the transformation or follow behind others.

Just like industrial corporations were not created top-down by government decree, the transformation of organizations toward innovative, knowledge-based, and networked partnerships will grow from below. Visionary leaders will inspire peers and other associates to break the rules of conventional business and jointly move their organizations into second cycles of innovation and growth. If you are such a visionary, I invite you to share your progress on my weblog, which you will find on www.thesecondcycle.com.

How Oticon Entered the Second Cycle

HOW I GOT INTO OTICON

Thursday, September 1, 1988, just before 10 A.M., I drove down the narrow Copenhagen Road, Klædemålet, to start my new job as CEO at hearing aid manufacturer Oticon. On the way to the office, I had wondered where to park the car because I knew the area was normally crammed with cars at that time of the day. But I had no reason to be concerned: Parking space number one, right next to the main entrance to the Oticon building, had been cleared for me, and a prominent sign showing my name and title had been put up.

More to my surprise, the chairman of the board and my predecessor were standing on the stairs, ready to welcome me to Oticon. They were dressed in perfect business attire, smiling and welcoming. And when we entered the building, the entire senior management team (about 20 people, most of them aged 50 and older) was waiting in the management's dining room to receive me. Champagne and petit fours were served, and the chairman and my predecessor gave speeches. I had to improvise one in which I thanked the board for the confidence it had shown in me by offering me this job. On my way home, I took the parking sign down and brought it home.

During my first month at Oticon, I couldn't really do much, because the board had decided that I needed an overlap period with my predecessor still in the chair. I had managed to negotiate that period down from six months to one month. So, I listened patiently to lengthy explanations about the industry, competition, the European Hearing Industry Manufacturer's Association, the largest customers, and Oticon's history, which dated back to 1904. Also described to me were the personality of the founder, Mr. William Demant, his family affairs, and why he donated shares in Oticon to a charitable foundation with the purpose to support the hearing impaired, the Oticon staff, and their families. I realized that during the first 84 years of company history, there had only been two CEOs before me. I was number three. Forty-two years average time as a CEO. That's continuity!

IN THE WRONG CORNER

Within that first month, I realized that Oticon was in much deeper trouble than I had thought when I accepted the job. I knew very well that Oticon was in financial trouble, but now I realized that there was more to the crisis than had met the eye initially:

- We were the highest cost manufacturer in the industry, whereas the market focused mostly on price.
- We made some of the world's largest hearing aids, whereas the market focused on cosmetics—that is, size.
- We were strong in stagnating northern Europe, whereas the market growth was concentrated in the U.S. and southern Europe.
- We were a medical equipment manufacturer that sold primarily to public hearing clinics, whereas the market was moving toward commercial chains of hearing aid dispensers.
- We were masters of standard behind-the-ear (BTE) hearing aids, whereas the market wanted custom-built in-the-ear (ITE) products.

- We stuck to analog technology, whereas the competition had just introduced digitally programmable products as a forerunner for fully digital sound processing hearing aids.
- Customers rightfully perceived Oticon as the arrogant we-know-better company.
- Our corporate culture was steeply hierarchical, conservative, and almost aristocratic, with a strong resistance to change.

We were in the wrong corner of the playing field, but why?

NOT OUR FAULT

I asked members of senior management why they thought we were in such trouble. They offered several different explanations:

- The U.S. dollar had fallen greatly against the European currencies—as much as 50 percent over four years from its peak in 1984. Oticon's cost base was primarily in northern Europe, which put our U.S. competitors at an "unfair advantage."
- The commercial hearing aid dispensers had persuaded patients to buy hearing aids according to size (cosmetics) rather than according to performance. Oticon maintained that it was unethical to sacrifice acoustical performance to cosmetics.
- Competition had managed to sell ITE hearing aids to patients that really would have been much better off with the larger and higher performing BTE products.
- Politicians and bureaucrats had focused on price instead of performance in the tenders that allocated hearing aid supply contracts to the important national hearing care schemes in the United Kingdom, Australia, Scandinavia, and other countries. Thus, Oticon had lost ground also in its key markets.

In short, it was other people's fault that Oticon was performing so terribly. And terrible it was. In 1987, the Oticon Group had lost DKK 41 million (Danish krone) (the equivalent to U.S. $7 million) on net sales of DKK 360 million ($52 million), a negative return on sales of some 11 percent. Equity stood at DKK 129 million ($22 million) after an aggressive revaluation of the company headquarters' buildings by some DKK 29 million ($5 million). The health of product and raw material stocks and debtors was still to be seen.

Cash flow was terrible. The banks had long lost confidence with Oticon, and I was "invited" to "status" meetings twice a month with the CEO of our primary bank. What an honor!

But company spirit was high: The lull would soon pass. The U.S. dollar would eventually rise, patients would again learn to appreciate sound quality instead of price, patients would get tired of small ITE hearing aids, and politicians would realize that hearing care was too important to squeeze financially.

I didn't believe it would ever pass.

THE TURNAROUND

Therefore, I instituted what I called a *purchasing sluice* a few days after I had taken the chair on October 1, 1988—no money could be spent, no financial commitment could be made, and no invoice could be paid without my prior personal authorization—no matter the size of the transaction. The only exception was sourcing of components according to approved production plans.

Staff members thought I was crazy. They thought that the whole company would close down. But I offered a 24-hour decision-making service: Any request that I had not rejected within 24 hours was automatically approved. So, the worst case scenario would be a 24-hour delay.

That taught me something about the business that I hadn't expected:

- High costs build up from hundreds of small transactions that management never sees.
- In a cash squeeze, many purchases can be delayed for months without affecting the business.
- The very control mechanism holds back unnecessary purchases quite efficiently.

The effect was dramatic. Within three months, Oticon became a net cash generator. The bank was surprised and proposed the status meetings to become monthly instead of twice a month. I happily accepted. Sometimes, I was even invited for lunch at the bank. The purchasing sluice was maintained for about 12 months.

During the first months, I could not figure out in which direction Oticon was focused. We did care about customers, but it appeared that we didn't agree who our customers were. The research department thought customers were the patients—that is, the hearing impaired. The sales and marketing departments thought that customers were the distributors around the world, including our 15 sales subsidiaries. The engineers in the technical department didn't really bother who the customer was; they felt that their job was to develop ever more advanced and higher performing hearing aids.

It struck me that no one at Oticon seemed to focus on the audiologist or the hearing aid dispenser that actually made most of the purchasing decisions on behalf of patients.

I figured that out through a series of visits to hearing clinics and dispensers around the world. They made it no secret that they loved the classical Oticon high-power BTE products, but they hated the company for its arrogance and conservatism. In the talks with audiologists, I followed a checklist that I had prepared based upon talks with my colleagues at head office. I decided to ask the audiologists which sort of car they thought of when looking upon Oticon versus the competition. The Oticon staff expected Oticon to be the BMW or Audis of the industry, perhaps Mercedes or Porsche. The audiologists, however, said that Oticon looked more like a London taxi or a VW bubble: proven, well-designed, old technology that runs for years. My staff thought I was joking when I reported back from my visits. Was I absolutely sure I had asked the right question? I had.

A NEW STRATEGY EMERGES

Shortly after my return from customer and distributor visits, I gathered senior management for a two-day workshop on the future direction of Oticon (November 18, 1988). At that point, less than two months after I had taken office, we reached consensus that Oticon needed to focus on the real customer: the person who dispenses (or fits) the hearing aid to the patient. And we changed terminology:

The *patient* became the *user*.

The *dispenser* became the *customer* or the *hearing care professional*.

In other words, we redefined our patients to become users or end users. We started to look upon customers not as ears, but as human beings. We needed to satisfy human needs instead of just audiological needs. We realized that our product was quality of life rather than amplification. We were no more just a medical equipment manufacturer. We became a hearing care business.

Later, we changed our motto as well. For decades, Oticon had called itself the "leaders in hearing technology," which fit reality well. The company had aimed to develop and manufacture the world's most advanced and highest performing hearing aids. But I wondered why I never met any consumer who asked for the world's most advanced hearing aids. Consumers inquired for smaller, more comfortable, more reliable, or simply cheaper products. In fact, I rarely met consumers that asked for hearing aids at all. They would rather avoid them. Consumers did not want better hearing. They just wanted to live a normal life with the hearing they had.

Therefore, we redefined Oticon's mission from "leaders in hearing technology" to "help[ing] people (with impaired hearing) to live as they wish with the hearing they have." Full stop. That made a major difference. Particularly because we used this new mission statement and the new focus on the hearing care professional (the customer) as the guideline for a badly needed downsizing of head office.

I personally went through every department in the head office to find out in what respect department members contributed to either making users happy or supporting the work of our customers (the hearing care professionals). Obviously, there were some departments that did not fit that mold (for example, the bookkeepers), but many other department members were simply unable to establish a proper link between their work and happy users or customers. These departments were closed down. This had two effects:

1. As the word spread, the remaining departments very rapidly became highly relevant for customers or users.

2. Those staff members that were not laid off could be moved into functions that added genuine value.

Head office staff was reduced by about 10 percent, sales started to grow, and the company turned profitable. Net operating income in 1989 reached an impressive DKK 28 million on DKK 469 million sales, equal to 6 percent return on sales. Not bad compared to –11 percent two years earlier.

Oticon was back on track.

BACK ON TRACK

The staff was happy. The board was happy.

I was unhappy. I felt that the fundamental problems had not yet been solved. We were still a high cost manufacturer, still strong in stagnating segments and markets, still technologically behind, still conservative and hierarchical, and still resistant to change. At least, we were temporarily profitable.

I doubted whether Oticon could survive as an independent company long term. After all, we were up against electronics giants such as Siemens, Philips, Sony, 3M, and others. They all had great competitive advantages due to their technology, manufacturing base, worldwide presence, and brands. And they made it no secret that they believed hearing aids would become a booming industry because of the demographic shift toward an aging population. They were prepared to invest. Oticon knew we needed to invest, but we had no money to invest.

PREPARING FOR REBIRTH

I was probably the only person in Oticon that had doubts about our ability to survive. But my doubts persisted.

That led me to perform a thorough, strategic analysis of Oticon's position and future. We couldn't afford consultants, but I studied value chains, competitive advantages and disadvantages, technological and market developments, and much more.

The analysis confirmed my first impression that Oticon was in deep trouble, despite the financial turn around. There was no way we could go on the way we were currently doing business. My conclusion was that our only chance to survive would be to fundamentally change corporate culture and behavior and to use this change to carry through a simultaneous upgrade of virtually every part of Oticon:

- We would build a brand new head office organization, which would include merging the commercial and technical departments that were located in separate buildings 20 kilometers apart. The mental distance was even greater.

- We would move distribution (in Copenhagen) closer to manufacturing (in Thisted, in northwest Jutland, 300 kilometers away) to be able to offer customized products and just-in-time deliveries to customers.

- We would build up an in-house chip design center to be able to develop the chips needed for future digital signal processors. Previously, we had bought chips from industry suppliers.

- We would build a new plant (in Thisted) to manufacture next generation digital signal processors that would build on a new technological platform. That would eventually free us from manufacturing in central Copenhagen where the workforce was expensive and less motivated.

- Last but not least, we would fundamentally change the way we worked as a company: from a rule-based, departmentalized, hierarchical engineering culture toward a customer-focused, flexible, innovative business culture.

In March 1989, we had a second workshop on strategy. Consensus was reached that we needed to carry through a massive change that would take several years before we could restore Oticon to its former grandeur. We also had to realize that we could not be everything to all customers. This led to a focus strategy. We would focus everything we did toward the *professional* dispenser. But what is a professional dispenser? We chose to define professionalism as dedication to continuously striving for better treatment efficiency. In other words, we started looking at dispensers that built their business on long-term end-user satisfaction.

Such focus would allow us to benefit from our "medical" background, but it would also require us to be very innovative and fast moving because this segment demanded rapid product innovation more than anything else. It also opened possibilities to offer a range of support services (dispenser systems) that were not directly linked to product.

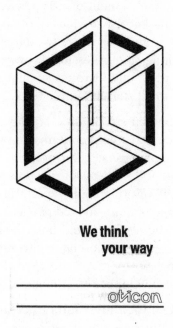

**We think
your way**

oticon

Figure A-1

I chose to communicate this strategy as a "sixth wave" in Oticon's development: We would have to become a service business. The six waves were the following:

1. Import of hearing aids from the U.S. for retail sale in Denmark (1904–1912).

2. Retailing extended to other countries in Scandinavia (1912–1943).

3. Build up small-scale production in Denmark and establish a network of distributors abroad (1943–1960).

4. Expand production to large scale and build network of sales subsidiaries (1960–1985).

5. Add ITE and commercial business focus to former BTE and medical focus (1985–1995).

6. Transforming the business from manufacturing into a service.

This led to the establishment of a dispenser systems business line to develop and market the services to the hearing care profession-al that were not product. We were to address the hearing care profession by thinking the professional's way. The plan was named "We think your way," and I wrote a small pamphlet about it, which was distributed to all staff in March 1989.

In late 1989, I invited a task force of staff to look into the idea of a new head office that would contain the two current head offices (technical and commercial). Enthusiasm was great, and shortly before Christmas 1989, the task force presented its proposals: several possible buildings that could be refurbished to our needs. The group felt that one building looked particularly attractive—a modern two-story building that could hold the technical departments on one floor and the commercial departments on the other floor. This would allow us to move the two parts of the head office together without much need to change the organization.

I almost exploded. I felt my efforts to create one single company out of the two parts of the head office had failed completely. Therefore, I decided to think it over during Christmas. This led me to write a four-page memo, which became known as, "Think the Unthinkable!" (in Danish, "Tænk det utænkelige!").

THINK THE UNTHINKABLE!

Despite optimism and good spirit in Oticon, this memo did not hit fertile ground. Senior management got it as a New Year's present upon returning from Christmas vacation. Most thought it was a joke. But the more resistance I had from the management team, the more I knew that this was exactly what Oticon needed. Endless discussions followed, but in early March 1990, I formally asked the board to approve the plan in principle, which it did. There was concern about financing, but that would depend on the price we could get for our existing headquarter building and the exact building we were to choose for the new headquarters. I decided to start the "Project 330" by inviting all headquarters' staff to a meeting on one of Denmark's most negative memorial days: April 18. I picked that day because it was the day Denmark lost South Jutland to Germany in 1864, a disaster for the nation. From there on, it could only be better. Likewise for Oticon: Now, we should start building our future. But which future? Here are the key points of the note "Think the Unthinkable" I sent out to all headquarters' staff on March 30, 1990:

> We are facing very tough competition; we have great competitive disadvantage, so we must "think the unthinkable," focusing on the professional dispenser and dramatically improving product development, manufacturing, reliability, supply chain management, marketing and sales support, and reducing administration costs.
>
> It costs us an average of DKK 440 to develop, manufacture, sell, and service one hearing aid. We need to reduce that number to DKK 300 in three years—that is, a 30 percent improvement in three years. Therefore, this project will be called Project 330.
>
> We will change the concept of a job to better match the talents of each individual. Everyone will have to do more than one job, including something he is not formally qualified to do (multijob).
>
> We will discontinue the current hierarchical departmental structure and substitute it by projects.

There will be project leaders to run projects, gurus to ensure a proper professional standard in everything we do, and mentors to help support every employee to do his best. All current job titles will have to go.

Ninety-five percent of all paper should go as well. We will install a state-of-the-art computer network that will allow every one of us to freely choose where to work every day. We will stimulate oral dialog and avoid writing memos to each other. Talking is more fun.

We will create an open and inspiring workplace with no walls or partitions. There will be plants and trees on wheels, perhaps 500 or 1,000 of them, to move around when we move from one project to another. We will create the most exciting and creative workplace in the country. It will be nothing like an ordinary office.

We will all need to understand not only what we do, but also how this fits into the overall picture. If everyone knows that, we will need less conventional management and control. This allows us to spend more time on tasks that benefit the customers.

To sum up: We will all do more of the things we like to do and we are good at. We will get rid of all barriers, and we will work as one big team. That will make us more valuable and in turn justify a higher salary.

It goes without saying that this six-page note gave rise to heavy discussion. I chose to break an unwritten rule by inviting staff to the April 18 meeting after the end of normal working hours—that is, at 4:00 P.M. No obligation to come. No payment for overtime.

THE NEW OTICON TAKES SHAPE

One hundred forty-three employees showed up out of about 150. There was total silence when I told my story about open offices with 1,000 trees and more. Afterwards, absolutely no questions whatsoever. But one secretary, Helle Thorup-Witt, dared stand up and ask for a show of hands: Who thought this project would be good for Oticon and who wanted to be part of it? I was just about paralyzed. What if no one or only very few were in favor? But the backing was massive. I guess some 80 percent of those present raised their hands. Senior management just sat there. Paralyzed. And while we had sandwiches and beer afterwards, there was an almost euphoric ambiance among the people that were present. Let's do it! It's going to be great fun!

Quickly, we established a project organization with groups to cope with the new information system, find an adequate building, design the new workplace, train everyone to use PCs, and so on. Participation in the project groups was open to all under the condition that we would all have to continue to perform our normal tasks anyway. Only the project leader, Steen Davidsen, worked full-time on the project.

I had expected that the massive backing from the staff would have calmed the resistance to the plan from senior management, but it didn't. There continued to be noise and resistance, and the only reply I could give was to invite those that were against the project to work full-time on running the existing business to make it stronger and leave the change project to the rest of us.

The situation was still far from stable, and I unfortunately helped screw things up myself.

My thesis at the Copenhagen Business School 10 years earlier had been an analysis of relocations of companies from Copenhagen to lower cost regions elsewhere in Denmark. One conclusion was that managers made location decisions emotionally and without properly analyzing and comparing alternatives. I strongly felt that I could not repeat that mistake myself. So, I initiated a search for proper locations for the new headquarters not only in Copenhagen, but also in the vicinity (that is, within a 100-kilometer distance) and in Jutland where we already had our main manufacturing location in Thisted. Most managers would probably have performed such an analysis in secrecy, but I chose to do it openly.

The Thisted option in particular seemed a dream opportunity to me. We could get an incredibly attractive fjord-side location and massive state funds to build a world-class new head office. We would be next to our biggest and most important production plant, which would shorten communication lines between research and development (R&D) and manufacturing. Housing and living costs were very low in Thisted, and we could even build our own marina right next to the factory. The natural beauty of the region was a great plus, and we would be heartily welcomed.

Wow, I thought. But few thought likewise. They felt we would be moving to land's end. They were afraid that the great personal savings on housing that would follow from moving to Thisted would be like a boomerang if they were ever to return to Copenhagen. I argued that they could simply put all the money they saved into the bank, which would more than allow them to return to Copenhagen whenever they wanted to. I sounded right, but most of the staff wasn't enthusiastic.

I lost the battle and realized that you can't win them all. Thisted was dropped as a possible location for the new head office.

Therefore, I looked at other attractive opportunities. I was particularly thrilled with a renaissance castle about 80 kilometers west of Copenhagen with a newly built state-of-the-art conference center. The whole property was for sale at very attractive terms. The local authorities of the region were dying to get us to move. Imagine what we could create at that spot. Cheaply. The architect's drawings looked fantastic. A dream project so close to Copenhagen. Most people would not have to move—at least short term. That looked like a winner to me.

But now the company was just about to explode. Danes are not very mobile—even 80 kilometers was perceived a very long distance. I realized that there was no more time for such analyses, and the following Thursday I looked through the classified ads for empty factory buildings in Copenhagen. I picked the best one that was available that week—the old Tuborg soft drink factory in the suburb of Hellerup, just north of Copenhagen—rented the building on a 10-year contract, and that was it.

Great relief followed. Now we knew where we were going. For years, many thought that the whole process was orchestrated to make everyone happy with my final choice. It wasn't.

Everything else was in transition. Not only did we prepare for the most fundamental change of the organization for 100 years, but we also built a new factory and distribution center in Thisted and prepared for a move of the distribution center from Copenhagen. The list of projects also included a new design center for integrated circuits, a new computerized tool shop, ISO 9001 certification, and the launch of three major breakthroughs: a separate business unit to partner with large commercial hearing care chains, a concept for an Oticon retail business, and the introduction of what became the world's first truly automatic hearing aid (MultiFocus).

In hindsight, it can be argued whether all these projects should have been carried through at one time. I think the following year's development of sales and profits prove that the plan was indeed what Oticon needed. Looking at how competition heated up in the years that followed, I doubt Oticon would have been alive had we not entered into this extremely aggressive change process. And fortunately, Oticon was a privately held company, which did not need to bother about short-term fluctuations in profit. The board took a five-year perspective and publicly announced in the annual report that Oticon was prepared to sacrifice short-term profits for long-term growth opportunities.

MAKING IT HAPPEN

It was nothing less than the rebirth of an 86-year-old company. I set the birth date to 8 A.M. on August 8, 1991. About 15 months after the memorable April 18 session. A date and time easy to remember for all. 8/8 at 8 A.M.

The change process was bumpy—particularly because the IT vendors backed out from our systems specification. They said it just couldn't be done; a fully electronic network with fully electronic storage of all incoming and internally generated documents was just too much for conventional IBM 386 computers, even with 20MB hard drives. At last, Andersen Consulting (now Accenture) and Hewlett Packard agreed to develop the solution, which was unlike anything they had seen before.

Today, the idea of establishing an almost paperless office where all document handling is fully electronic and where staff can freely move from one desk to the other without bringing all their paper files seems ordinary. However, even today, 15 years after the Oticon revolution, the majority of companies I know still have great piles of paper everywhere. This is despite the fact that today's ordinary mobile phone has more memory and processor capacity than the high performance Oticon workstations at that time.

In 1990, five years before the Internet took off and even longer before anyone spoke of portable computers, the idea of a full-scale paperless office was truly revolutionary. It sounded surrealistic, and it became front-page news in major media all over the world. Most people outside Oticon were convinced it would never work, but one person had the courage to do it: Torben Petersen, a recognized authority in nuclear reactor design that I had come to know five years before at the Risoe National Laboratory. I hired Torben as Oticon's IT project manager, and he and his team wrote IT history by managing this extremely ambitious project on time and budget.

Only 10 percent to 15 percent of Oticon staff members had ever used a PC. In a few months' time, the whole company would be entirely dependent upon PC and network use. Time and money was extremely scarce. There was no way we could afford to carry through the necessary education and training program for all staff. We were stuck. But that led us to design a new deal. Every staff member would pay a modest amount to get a brand new PC just before Christmas 1990 to use at home with all the relevant software and all the computer games we could possibly buy. The employee would then take care of her own PC training in her free time. Employees would help each other with the training.

That worked. Almost everyone accepted the home PC offer, which meant that all staff was prepared for the new system. In addition, all staff became flexible to do work at the times that fit their schedule. Families and friends became excited about Oticon and our change process. It suddenly became attractive to work for Oticon.

However, uncertainty remained great. What would happen to the incoming mail? Would we continue to keep paper files after documents had been scanned into the system? I argued no, but few people believed me. We needed to show that we meant it. Why not visualize it physically? So we did: We located the mailroom at the very center of the building at the first floor. In that room, we set up our good old shredder, which got new paint to look more up-to-date. Below the shredder, we installed a big glass tube, which took the confetti down through the company restaurant to the recycling container in the basement. The glass tube allowed staff members to watch the shredded paper fall gently like snow while they enjoyed lunch at the restaurant. That turned out to be a very good investment, which paid itself back about a thousand times because all major international television stations featured that tube in their reports about this new crazy company. The staff started to believe that the rebirth could be done.

I learned that symbols are important, also in business. Think the Unthinkable became a symbol not only of Project 330, but a motto for Oticon. We translated it into Latin and carved "*Cogitate Incognita*" into one of the columns in the reception area of the new head office.

But what was to happen with all the expensive Danish design office furniture in the old buildings? Not to forget the antiques in the executive offices. In the new building, there would only be simple desks without drawers and a caddy to hold a few files and personal items. Managers in particular wanted to bring their large desks, sofas, lamps, and antique clocks to the new office.

That reminded me about the concepts of learning and un-learning. To allow for learning a new skill, you must often spend time to de-learn your old habits. That analogy could well be applied for the furniture issue. Therefore, I announced that all furniture from the old headquarters' buildings would be put at an auction for all staff to buy at a date no later than 30 days from D-day (August 8, 1991). And everything would be on view for the last three months before we moved. Simply enter the office of your boss, take a look at his furniture, and decide how much you would like to pay for it! That helped shake up the old habits and structures.

Suddenly, no one wanted to bring his office furniture to the new building after the option arose to buy it cheaply for home use. The auction lasted about eight hours, and it was an experience I will not forget. Not only because I managed to buy my own executive desk very reasonably, but also because the very selling of the furniture was a symbolic act where we all said goodbye to the past. That day, Oticon passed the point of no return.

In the design of the new head office, we were concerned that the new organizational design could lead to too many meetings. If we did not have traditional managers, would the staff waste its time sitting down and talking instead of getting things done?

Figure A-2

We came up with two ideas that may sound pretty ordinary today, but which created a lot of noise in 1991: the meeting rooms without tables and the meeting places without chairs.

We had noted the old truth that participants in meetings tend to sit at the same chairs and to build up positions by their location at the table. We also tended to hide behind our papers (and later, laptop PCs) to protect our position and status. That observation inspired us to try meeting rooms without tables and without specific positions. Only a round sofa in which everybody could just sit down as they wanted in a relaxed manner. No table was needed because we had virtually no paper (the paperless office).

That made a great difference. Meetings became more dynamic, more fun, and shorter, and it was obvious that participants became more flexible and willing to give up their status and traditional views in the process of finding new solutions.

The meeting places without chairs worked even better. We designed those where meetings could be held standing around the coffee bar. Whiteboards and computers helped stimulate creativity and focus the process.

I don't know today if it was the new types of meeting rooms or other factors that contributed most to the apparent increase in both employee satisfaction and efficiency. Prior to designing the new office, we did a survey to find out how our engineers in the product development department were spending their time. I had a suspicion that they didn't even use 50 percent of their time on genuine product development work. Administration, meetings, reports, and other tasks tended to take up their time. We were shocked: The survey indicated that the correct figure was not 50 percent, but rather 25 percent. Only one out of four hours was spent doing genuine product development work. The rest of the time was not wasted, but it was used on activities that only indirectly contributed to making customers happier. Those survey results gave me confidence that, even if some of our ideas did not work, we could only improve our time management.

The open office, the meeting places, the information system, and the flexible organization all aimed at increasing communication, flexibility, creativity, and speed of work. But we realized some tasks do not benefit from increased communication and interaction. Therefore, we established five *study cells*, which could only be booked for one day at a time. The study cell was a small office with a computer and not much more. I went there one or two times per month when I had to write reports to the board, strategy documents, and so on. Nothing to disturb you whatsoever!

FINANCING

Financing the whole project remained an issue. The old head office was overvalued and no one wanted to pay the sales price we had assumed. Contractors were already building in Thisted. Machines for the new tool shop had to be ordered. Engineers were already on training for the new chip design centre. A recent introduction of a new line of ITE instruments for the U.S. was a logistics nightmare. Cash flow had again turned negative due to investments and time and money spent on all the changes. The board was increasingly nervous, and discussions went back and forth on whether to stop the whole thing. I maintained that negative cash flow in a period of heavy investments and total change was according to plan and should be no surprise. I argued that there were only minor deviations from the already approved plans, but perhaps the board had not fully realized the extent of what they had approved. Pressure mounted, and I suggested that the board invite management and staff to make a personal investment in the company. I personally would be prepared to invest a major amount, and I believed the rest of the staff would also be quite willing to participate.

The board was extremely skeptical. I believe they never thought we could raise the money, and therefore they gave an okay to the following deal: The board would ask our banks to set a fair market value for the business. I would invest some DKK 26 million ($4 million), which I would have to borrow, at fair market value. The management would be invited to subscribe about DKK 5 million ($1 million) at the same valuation, and staff would be offered a similar amount with 33 percent and 50 percent discounts according to salary levels and seniority. In other words, the highest paid would be allowed to invest more, but at a higher price.

I managed miraculously to borrow the money with some help from my brother Peder, the rest of the management responded positively as well, and the staff was enthusiastic. Every single share was subscribed, and the company had sufficient funding to carry through the Project 330 processes. Non-executive board members were offered the possibility to invest at fair market value as well, including the employee representatives at the board. The employee representatives were mostly union people, who were now put in a delicate dilemma. Should they invest like managers and risk to become capitalists instead of union representatives? They put the issue to a vote among members and received an overwhelming yes. Of course, they should invest if they wanted to! Why not? The share issue was carried through late 1990 and was followed up by new employee share schemes at regular intervals.

That turned out to be a good decision, both from the employees' point of view and for the company. Imagine what you can do in a company where everyone is in the same boat, including the union members?

The driving force from the union side was the representatives from the Thisted factory. Thisted is a small town located in a somewhat remote area of Denmark—almost as far from Copenhagen as you can go. Thisted was chosen as a manufacturing location about 25 years earlier, mainly because there were generous government subsidies to move out production from Copenhagen to the less developed regions of the country. The plant had performed much better than expected and production manager Lars Kirk had managed to build a strong team with an excellent cooperation between unions and management. Gradually, the majority of Oticon staff became located in Thisted. This gave the Thisted employees control over the election of employee representatives to the board. The cooperative spirit from Thisted spilled over to the board.

A GOOD STORY

Did I ever doubt we would succeed? Never, really! I was so sure this would work that not only did I dare to borrow a fortune to invest in Oticon at the most critical moment in the process, but I also chose to share information about the process with other companies and the general public through a project, The Company of the Future, organized in cooperation with the Danish Industries Association.

The Company of the Future project obliged Oticon to share experiences from the change process with other businesses through regular information and conferences. About four months before the new organization was to be implemented in the new head office, we held a small press conference to share our plans with whoever wanted to hear.

Not many journalists showed up at the press conference, but the response was overwhelming. In the weeks that followed, almost every newspaper in the country had big articles about The Company of the Future. The new flexible workplace was called a *spaghetti organization* because it had no obvious structure, with every employee interacting freely with all others. Readers often thought that the new organization had already been physically implemented and much confusion followed. Family, friends, and neighbors asked questions to our employees. I remember one skeptical secretary who told me that because she had explained the new organization and the flexible office so many times to family and friends, she had started to believe it could be done.

D-day, August 8, 1991, approached. At 8.00 A.M., the doors were opened to The Company of the Future. To our great surprise, major international media, such as CNN, had found their way to Hellerup to cover the rebirth of what they saw as one of the craziest companies they could imagine.

We did it!

The media went crazy. Oticon became the company story of the year, and reporters, students and their teachers, union people, consultants, HR managers, and the like flooded us. We received more than 5,000 visitors every year in a very small head office that covered less than 4,000 square meters. Employees felt they were in a zoo. It was unavoidable that exaggerations occurred when wildly enthusiastic journalists wrote their cover stories on this miracle in Hellerup. That gave us problems internally. Staff could not always recognize the wildly enthusiastic stories. I tried to handle this by allowing journalists to speak freely with any employee they met, but that made the problem even bigger.

My colleagues in the Board of the Danish Industries Association did not share the enthusiasm of the media. Would we ever make money? Was this serious business or a media flop? Was I serious when I said that managers should not stick to their constitutional right to make decisions, but rather look upon leadership as an obligation? Would the middle managers ever accept positions that didn't carry titles or offices? What about company cars? And did I not have an office? How could we keep things secret? Would competition not steal all our company secrets? How could any bank be stupid enough to lend me money for such an investment? And what would I do for the staff members that had invested, if things went wrong?

Very few of my colleagues asked what they could learn from the experiment, simply because they were convinced it would never work.

It worked.

MORE DIFFICULTIES

We were not without problems, however. It took time to adjust to the new reality—particularly for the former middle managers. They knew that they had no longer had subordinates, but many didn't accept it. So they continued to manage, plan, control, and direct their former employees. But the employees did what they wanted to. Conflicts were inevitable.

One day, a former middle manager came to me to discuss this point. We sat down in one of the small discussion rooms, and he openly admitted that he didn't know what to do as a department head in this so-called spaghetti organization. I asked him to tell me what his current salary was. After he had hesitantly given the figure, I told him that he was probably the highest paid employee I had ever met that didn't know what to do for his company. Silence. He realized that he would have basically three options:

1. Return to the specialist function that he had performed prior to becoming a manager.
2. Find an adequate project and become a project leader.
3. Become a mentor (people manager) who took responsibility to coach and support a number of staff members. These members voluntarily would have to choose him as their mentor.

After long silence, he opted to return to the specialist role. He admitted that when he had been promoted to department head, the company had lost a good specialist, and it had gotten a bad leader in return. Now, the time had come to reverse this process. He spent many happy years at Oticon after that day, and he even made more money.

Salaries became an issue. If there is no formal hierarchy, who should then be paid higher? Should everybody be paid equally? The engineers' union was particularly concerned. It became clear to me that we would have to abandon all existing pay scales for salaried staff. Instead of defining a new set of pay scales, we designed a system for ongoing adjustment of salaries. The following is the five-step procedure:

1. The mentor or people manager, who has been chosen by the employee, invites the employee to a short meeting where the employee explains to the mentor how she has made a contribution to Oticon's business during the last 12 months. Everything counts.

2. The mentor then performs a reality check by openly talking to the employee's colleagues about their perception of the employee in question.

3. The mentor then looks into company files and industry statistics to determine his recommended pay rise or pay reduction for the following 12 months.

4. Mentors meet once a month to decide by consensus how the salary of each individual employee up for review this month (that is, about one twelfth of all staff) shall be adjusted.

5. The mentor again meets with the employee to explain the outcome of the process. If the employee is dissatisfied with the adjustment, he has no right of appeal other than the possibility to choose another mentor for next year's review.

After quite some noise in the transition process, this system gradually made salary adjustments a non-issue at Oticon. Everyone agreed that the system was fair, and the adjustments gradually led to more differentiated salaries in which genuine-to-high performers were paid accordingly. Low performers or employees that had clearly been overpaid were gradually moved downward to adequate salary levels.

The change process taught us a paradox: The more freedom of execution we as a company want to give to staff, the more clarity we must create about mission, vision, strategy, and values. We had clarified mission, vision, and strategy, but we were not really sure what our values were.

To clarify values, I wrote a draft note, in which I spelled out what we as a management team basically believed (assumptions) about our staff, what we would do to implement the consequences of those assumptions in the real world (execution), and what we expected from staff in return (expectations).

For example, we as a management team assume that Oticon's employees want to be treated as autonomous human beings. They will take responsibility whenever we allow them to do so (assumption). Therefore, we will agree upon clear goals and directions for work in order to allow employees to plan and execute their tasks. We will spend minimum resources on control. If possible, each employee will define his own job tasks, working hours, and workplace (execution). In return, we expect each individual staff member to take responsibility and actually do his best (expectations).

We ended up describing assumptions, execution, and expectations within eight aspects of work at Oticon: responsibility, development, freedom, understanding, growth, partnership, feedback, and security.[1] The note was distributed to all staff and became subject to what we called a *dialog shop*, where all staff worked together for a full day (a Saturday, not a working day!) discussing and refining what we called our basic human values.[2] The discussions helped create consensus among staff, and we realized that the more we all agreed about the basic values and beliefs, the better we could do without traditional managers. The dialog shop was repeated every other year to refresh our minds and to make sure new employees fully understood our values.

---

[1] In the toolbox section in this book you can find assumptions, execution, and expectations in detail for the eight areas of work at Oticon.

[2] The mechanics of a "dialogue shop" can be found in the toolbox section later in the book: CCCP Consensus Creation Crash Program.

MULTIFOCUS—THE FIRST COMMERCIAL BREAKTHROUGH

Neither a new head office nor a new procedure for adjusting salaries will sell hearing aids. But the spaghetti organization stimulated creativity across the board. We were in desperate need of something new for the big industry fairs in October/November 1991. The pipeline had nothing to offer.

The project leader of an R&D project that had recently been closed down, the so-called E36 BTE hearing aid project, approached me in June 1991 and proposed that we take a second look at it.

Ten years earlier, E36 had been designed to fit into a product generation that was now in the process of being phased out. The hearing aid was big, had an old-fashioned design, used old analog technology, was expensive to produce, and the novel nonlinear amplification concept did not make anybody outside of the R&D department enthusiastic. Moreover, it would require Oticon to teach the hearing care professionals to adjust the hearing aid according to a different formula than they were used to. The salespeople had not been happy about that. It looked pretty much like born loser.

But, with a small spaghetti group, I was desperate enough to take a second look at the product. Two things surprised us. Users that had field tested the product were very happy with the sound. They particularly liked the speech intelligibility in noise, which the nonlinear amplification system in E36 produced. And one young engineer noted that in most of the instruments that came back from field tests, the volume controls had not been touched. They were still at factory settings.

We looked at each other. Wow! Had we designed the world's first fully automatic hearing aid without really knowing it? I believed we had, and the same day, I wrote a letter to the project team and expressed confidence that we could finally get E36 flying. Whoever wanted to join this effort were welcome. We were in desperate hurry to get it ready for an October launch.

The team was enthusiastic. Together, we discovered that E36 could be viewed as a parallel to the evolution of new generations of spectacles: At first, all spectacles were just one focal length—that is, monofocal. Later, bifocal lenses were invented. That saved users from having to change between two sets of spectacles for distance and reading use. And now we have multifocal lenses that gradually adapt focus to the need of the user. Wasn't that exactly what E36 was doing? A multifocal hearing aid. So why not call E36 MultiFocus?

Field tests to confirm the automatic operation were successful, and the necessary documentation for the new fitting method was tested. But the instrument was still very big and had an old-fashioned design. Why not learn from Danish hi-fi equipment maker Bang & Olufsen? Let's make the shell matte gray like brushed aluminum. And why not put the MultiFocus logo on it to be clearly seen? Why shouldn't users be proud of their hearing aids instead of hiding them? Let's position this product as the first hearing aid that was designed to be seen, not to be hidden!

But E36 was still damn big. Would anyone even consider trying it?

Why not make it appear smaller? Let's make the world's largest hearing aid package! It can contain an innovative user instruction video where we can demonstrate the unique benefits of MultiFocus compared to all other hearing aids, even the digitally programmable ones from competition. And, let us make a diary to help the user experience the unique sound in different listening environments and report back to the audiologist. If the package is large, the hearing aid will look smaller. At least we may get users to try it.

But pricing was an issue. The rest of the E30 series was currently being discounted as normally in the last phase of the product life-cycle. Could we maintain the normal price level? We certainly could. We actually decided to go beyond the original E30 price level by increasing it another 50 percent to match the price level of digitally programmable hearing aids from competition. Although the technology was old, we knew we had a better product from the user's point of view. Why not show it by pricing MultiFocus at a premium? Our sales staff was nervous. The product was 10 years old. But we decided that the fact that E36 was 10 years old only reflected that Oticon had been 10 years ahead of time. Why should that disqualify the product?

The introduction package broke with everything Oticon and the industry had done before. Marketing messages did not speak about acoustical performance, decibel, and frequencies:

Introducing MultiFocus. A New Dimension in Hearing Care.

MultiFocus. Because Sound—like the Earth—isn't flat.

The Sensation of MultiFocus. It goes to the heart of what hearing is all about.

The industry had never seen anything like that product introduction in October 1991. It came as a complete surprise from the company no one would have expected it from. Users were surprised and accepted MultiFocus despite its size. Professionals had been looking for something really new for years. Something that would offer their customers genuine user benefits. Fully automatic operation. No volume control to fiddle with. Superior speech intelligibility in noise. Of course, an advanced product like that has to be big! Wow!

Figure A-3

MultiFocus more than paid for all the investments in the transformation process in Oticon during the following two to three years. But short term, we were pressed. Demand for MultiFocus was many times higher than anybody had dreamed of. Expensive brochures, video, diary, and packaging had to be produced quickly in multiple languages before we could start selling. Cash flow suffered.

Despite my reports of overwhelming customer interest in MultiFocus, the board was losing confidence in me and requested that I find a chief financial officer who could "restore order" in the house. I argued that the house was certainly in good order, the timing was wrong, and we should wait another six months, but the board gave me no choice. Either I found a CFO myself, or the board would do it for me.

MANAGEMENT OF SPAGHETTI

I was furious, but I chose the first option and found Niels Jacobsen. Niels was my exact opposite. Very structured and financially oriented. Whenever I saw opportunities, he helped me see threats. Whenever I went for expansion, he helped balance cash flow and profitability. We chose not to have a formal division of labor, and we agreed to base our cooperation on consensus decision-making, although I was formally the CEO. We got to know each other so well that we could make decisions on each other's behalf. What started very negatively became a lucky combination and a very good decision, despite my initial resistance.

MultiFocus was only the beginning. In the following years, Oticon floated the market with new products and other innovations that took competition by surprise: a hearing care program for children (Otikids), a color scheme that allowed users to match the color of the hearing aid to the hair color instead of the skin colors used by the rest of the industry, new counseling tools, and more. Competition fought us fiercely—in particular, one of our Danish competitors, which had very successfully introduced a digitally programmable (analog) product as early as 1988. The competitor argued that a fully automatic hearing aid was close to an impossible thought until they finally introduced one themselves a few years later. A German company introduced Multifon, and others imitated our marketing. We were flattered.

Innovation not only affected products and services toward customers. Oticon's entire business system was streamlined and rationalized due to better communication, direct contact between staff from different functions, and a transparent electronic communication between production and logistics in Thisted, the head office in Copenhagen, and the increasing number of sales companies around the world.

ISO CERTIFIED CHAOS

The ISO 9001 (Europe) and FDA GMP (U.S.) quality management certification projects, however, ran into difficulties. There was a 180-degree conflict between the rigid requests from inspectors to structure every detail of every thing and Oticon's flexible, unhierarchical business philosophy. We rejected job descriptions and the very concept of a quality handbook in paper form. Why should this be our only paper-based publication when everything else had become electronic? After hundreds of hours of work and lengthy negotiations, we finally agreed on the certification—perhaps the world's first and only ISO certified chaos?

It came as no surprise to me that the 1991 year-of-change accounts showed only a modest operating profit for the Oticon Group of some DKK 9 million based on sales of DKK 477 million, a modest 2 percent return on sales. But then things took off. Due to MultiFocus sales in particular, and new products and services in general, sales grew 13 percent and 23 percent the next two years with profitability soaring to return on sales levels of 6 percent and 13 percent, respectively.

READY FOR THE DIGITAL AGE

Early 1992, we were finally ready to enter the digital race—that is, the race for a fully digital signal processor that would add genuine benefits to users and hearing care professionals. We were probably three to eight years behind the industry leaders. We didn't even have a digitally programmable (analog) product to match the products that competitors such as Bernafon and Widex had launched in 1988.

We chose to use the spaghetti organization to its limits by forming a project group for this Jump project that included all necessary capabilities. Jump got first priority, and the team worked day and night to make it reality. Fortunately, the Oticon research center had worked with researchers at Linköping University in Sweden to develop and field test the fitting algorithm for the future processor, so we knew we were on solid ground. We knew we could provide real substance to users, not only digital technology. Despite problems and errors along the road, the project progressed rapidly. We opted for a relatively complicated design, splitting incoming sound into 16 channels that could be programmed for individual response. This made the chip somewhat big and forced us to compromise by splitting the development into two phases: a behind-the-ear (BTE) product with an in-the-ear (ITE) product to follow one year later.

Part of the share purchase deal with management and staff in 1990 was that Oticon would go public after five years—that is, 1995. We went public in May 1995. Although we could have boosted the Initial Public Offering (IPO) price significantly had we waited to go public after the announcement of our fully digital product, we chose to keep Jump in the pocket until after the IPO, which took place on the Copenhagen Stock Exchange. That spring, we worked day and night. We had just acquired the Swiss competitor Bernafon earlier that year. Much work needed to be done integrating the supply chain of the two companies, and on top, we had to do the IPO. Plus run the business, of course. Again, the spaghetti structure helped us. Many staff members helped in these projects along with their normal work. That allowed us to carry through everything with virtually no additional resources.

Meanwhile, sales and profits soared. 1994 sales grew by another 13 percent, and profits were up 55 percent, which gave us an 18 percent return on sales. Return on equity reached an impressive 39 percent. Ready to go!

Skepticism from managers from other companies—including com-petition—remained all the way up to the IPO. We were blunt and chose as our tagline for the IPO: "Oticon introduces knowledge on the Copenhagen Stock Exchange." Hot air said the skeptics. But subscriptions from investors were overwhelming and at the IPO price level we chose, we had seven times over subscription. If we had chosen to double the price, shares would still have been four times over subscribed. But we were more focused on life after the IPO, making sure that the investors that had shown us such con-fidence would see their shares go up.

Oticon had entered the premier league.

In the summer of 1995, we were getting ready to launch our first fully digital product, the DigiFocus. During the three and one half years of development, we had constantly expected competition to launch their first digital products. We couldn't imagine that Oticon would ever be number one. After all, we had probably started eight years later than several competitors. So how could we ever win the race? We had set high levels of ambition; we would not launch a fully digital hearing aid just because of technology. There had to be genuine user benefits.

In August, we decided to go. If we managed to come first, the launch of the world's first "computer at the ear" would be a sensa-tion. We realized that outside help for the launch was necessary. A large multinational communications agency submitted a glossy proposal that didn't make me happy. It reminded me of the strat-egy of winning a war through an overwhelming show of force. It was very expensive and not very smart. It would be much better to try to win through an unconventional and unexpected surprise attack. A newly established local communications group, Sigma, became our partner. Sigma founder, Klaus Fog, cross-examined every one of us to make sure that the product had substance. He was highly surprised to hear how academics from Sweden and the U.S. praised the power of the concept. Academic endorsement became the backbone of the launch: "The world's first computer at the ear" became the catch line, whereas academic endorsement and user testimonials provided the substance.

We chose London as the venue for the launch, and Sigma managed to get most major international media to come for the event.

Media response exceeded anything even the largest Danish companies have ever experienced at product launch. Consumers in all continents heard the story of the computer at the ear and how technology could benefit the hearing impaired. Hearing care professionals all over the world were bombarded with questions, and despite a massive communications effort, we got some badwill for not preparing the retail sector well enough. Still worse was the fact that we were hit by last-minute technical problems in the process of scaling up production. Backorder lists skyrocketed, and competition managed to create an impression that Oticon had launched DigiFocus too early just to be first.

I don't think that is a fair conclusion. We knew that DigiFocus was a sensation, both within the industry and for Oticon as a publicly traded company. We had reached a point where the risk of DigiFocus news spreading to the investment community was becoming too high. We had no other choice than simply to tell the news to the general public. It is impossible to pre-announce such news to prepare the trade weeks in advance.

The Danish public hearing care service was particularly angry. They criticized Oticon that we had not chosen Denmark as the launch pad, and they could not accept that all Danish hearing clinics had not been informed weeks in advance to cope with requests from patients. In addition, Oticon's high profile meant that knowledge about and interest for hearing aids in general was increasing. The Danes in particular now realized that hearing aids were no more just bulky amplifiers, but rather high-tech computers. That inspired many people to finally see their doctor about some help with their hearing, which in turn led to much increased demand for public hearing service. The public hearing clinics were very critical against us for creating interest for hearing help. They became busier, and their budgets were under pressure. We did not do well at our home market in that period.

But the project team—and most other Oticon staff—worked its way through the problems, and DigiFocus became an established market leader contributing greatly to Oticon's continued growth after 1995.

LIFE IN THE PREMIER LEAGUE

Following DigiFocus, Oticon sales and profits continued to grow rapidly. Ambitions to compete in all segments of the hearing care market called for expansion of the head office organization. The spaghetti organization that had worked well for a total of about 150 staff at head office had to be adjusted. We chose to divide the marketing and product development activities into three business teams that would focus on the mass market, the mid-price, and the high performance segments. We set up a technology team to support the three business teams.

Although this introduced some structure into the spaghetti, the basic concept remained the same, and all teams continued to work side-by-side in one big workspace. I was constantly met with questions about spaghetti that had now turned into lasagna. But to me, the change was both natural and necessary, and subsequent company performance confirmed that it served the purpose well. To our surprise, the spaghetti organization gradually made its way to Oticon companies throughout the world; Sweden, Norway, Germany, Switzerland, The Netherlands, France, Spain, U.S., Australia, and New Zealand all implemented their own versions of the spaghetti organization. Italy was limited by its historic house in Florence, and Japan did not really see any reason to adapt. To our even greater surprise, the company we took over in 1995, Bernafon in Switzerland, went enthusiastically ahead to set up its own spaghetti organization. It turned out that the spaghetti concept blended very well with the Swiss culture.

I chose to leave Oticon shortly before my 10-year anniversary in 1998. I felt the company was in good shape; the next generation management was ready to take over under the leadership of Niels Jacobsen, and the product pipeline gave me confidence that Oticon would continue to perform well in the years to come. Performance has actually been even better than I expected. From D-day 1991 until I left Oticon in 1998, annual sales had grown by an average of 19 percent from DKK 477 million to DKK 1613 million, including the Bernafon acquisition. From 1998 to 2003, the growth has continued at the same impressive rate of about 19 percent per year including some acquisitions. Return on sales reached 15.4 percent in 1998, up from 1.8 percent in 1991. Profitability has continued to increase after 1998, hitting an all time high of 23.3 percent in 2004.

Oticon is well into its second cycle.

INDEX

F

G

H

I

N

W–Z

Ideas. Action. Impact.
**Wharton School
Publishing**

Kenichi Ohmae
THE NEXT GLOBAL STAGE
Challenges and Opportunities in Our Borderless World

Mukul Pandya, Robbie Shell, Susan Warner, Sandeep Junnarkar, Jeffrey Brown
NIGHTLY BUSINESS REPORT PRESENTS LASTING LEADERSHIP
What You Can Learn from the Top 25 Business People of Our Times

C. K. Prahalad
THE FORTUNE AT THE BOTTOM OF THE PYRAMID
Eradicating Poverty Through Profits

Michael A. Roberto
WHY GREAT LEADERS DON'T TAKE YES FOR AN ANSWER
Managing for Conflict and Consensus

Arthur Rubinfeld, Collins Hemingway
BUILT FOR GROWTH
Expanding Your Business Around the Corner or Across the Globe

Scott A. Shane
FINDING FERTILE GROUND
Identifying Extraordinary Opportunities for New Ventures

Oded Shenkar
THE CHINESE CENTURY
The Rising Chinese Economy and Its Impact on the Global Economy, the Balance of Power, and Your Job

David Sirota, Louis A. Mischkind, and Michael Irwin Meltzer
THE ENTHUSIASTIC EMPLOYEE
How Companies Profit by Giving Workers What They Want

Thomas T. Stallkamp
SCORE!
A Better Way to Do Busine$$: Moving from Conflict to Collaboration

Glen Urban
DON'T JUST RELATE — ADVOCATE!
A Blueprint for Profit in the Era of Customer Power

Craig M. Vogel, Jonathan Cagan, and Peter Boatwright
THE DESIGN OF THINGS TO COME
How Ordinary People Create Extraordinary Products

Yoram (Jerry) Wind, Colin Crook, with Robert Gunther
THE POWER OF IMPOSSIBLE THINKING
Transform the Business of Your Life and the Life of Your Business

An Invitation from the Editors:
Join the
Wharton School Publishing Membership Program

Dear Thoughtful Executive,

We hope that you've discovered valuable ideas in this book, which will help you affect real change in your professional life. Each of our titles is evaluated by the Wharton School Publishing editorial board and earns the Wharton Seal of Approval — ensuring that books are timely, important, conceptually sound and/or empirically based and — key for you — implementable.

We encourage you to join the Wharton School Publishing Membership Program. Registration is simple and free, and you will receive these and other valuable benefits:

- **Access to valuable content** — receive access to additional content, including audio summaries, articles, case studies, chapters of forthcoming books, updates, and appendices.
- **Online savings** — save up to 30% on books purchased everyday at Whartonsp.com by joining the site.
- **Exclusive discounts** — receive a special discount on the Financial Times and FT.com when you join today.
- **Up to the minute information** — subscribe to select Wharton School Publishing newsletters to be the first to learn about new releases, special promotions, author appearances, and events.

Becoming a member is easy; please visit Whartonsp.com and click "Join WSP" today.

Wharton School Publishing welcomes your comments and feedback. Please let us know what interests you, so that we can refer you to an appropriate resource or develop future learning in that area. Your suggestions will help us serve you better.

Sincerely,

Jerry Wind
windj@wharton.upenn.edu

Tim Moore
tim_moore@prenhall.com

Become a member today at Whartonsp.com

Why Great Leaders Don't Take Yes for an Answer
Managing for Conflict and Consensus
BY MICHAEL A. ROBERTO

Executives hear "yes" far too often. Their status and power inhibits c...
did dialogue. They don't hear bad news until it's too late. They get gro...
think, not reality. They think they've achieved consensus, then find th...
decisions undermined or derailed by colleagues who never really bou...
in. They become increasingly isolated; even high-risk or illegal actic...
can begin to go unquestioned. Inevitable? Absolutely not. In this bo...
Harvard Business School Professor Michael Roberto shows you how...
promote honest, constructive dissent and skepticism...use it to impro...
your decisions...and then align your entire organization to fully supp...
the decisions you make. Drawing on his extensive research on execu...
decision-making, Roberto shows how to test and probe the members...
your management team...discover when "yes" means "yes" and whe...
doesn't...and build real, deep consensus that leads to action. Along...
way, Roberto offers important new insights into managing teams, miti...
ing risk, promoting corporate ethics through effective governance, a...
much more. Your organization and your executive team have imme...
untapped wisdom: this book will help you tap that wisdom to the fulle...

ISBN 0131454390, © 2005, 304 pp., $26.95

Making Innovation Work
How to Manage It, Measure It, and Profit from It
BY TONY DAVILA, MARC J. EPSTEIN, AND ROBERT SHELTON

You have to be dynamic and innovative to stay a step ahead of the competition—sometimes, in fact, just to stay in business! But profitable innovation doesn't just 'happen.' It must be managed, measured, executed on...and too few companies know how to do that well. Now, for the first time, Making Innovation Work presents a formal innovation process proven to work at HP, Microsoft and Toyota, to help ordinary managers drive top and bottom line growth from innovation. To write this book, the authors have drawn on their unsurpassed innovation consulting experience—as well as the most thorough review of innovation research ever performed. They'll show you what works, what doesn't, and how to use all your management tools to dramatically increase the payoff from your innovation investments. You'll learn how to define the right strategy effective innovation; how to structure your organization to innovate best; how to implement management systems to assess ongoing innovation; how to incentivize your team to deliver, and much more. And, since "you can't manage what you can't measure," this book offers the first authoritative guide to using metrics at every step of the innovation process—from idea creation and selection through prototyping and commercialization. Innovation isn't magic, but it can be. Innovation is more critical than ever. Now discover how to deliver it—consistently, and join the ranks of the high-performing companies that are making headlines.

ISBN 0131497863, © 2006, 368 pp., $29.99

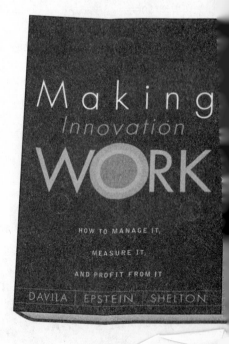